A Healing Year

DAILY MEDITATIONS FOR LIVING WITH LOSS

D1262547

Text © 2000 by Alaric Lewis, O.S.B.
Published by One Caring Place
Abbey Press
St. Meinrad, Indiana 47577

Library of Congress Catalog Number
00-103688

ISBN 0-87029-346-X

Printed in the United States of America

A Healing Year

DAILY MEDITATIONS FOR LIVING WITH LOSS

By Alaric Lewis, O.S.B.

One Caring Place

Abbey Press

This book is dedicated
to the memory of
my mother, Shirley Jean Lewis.

Introduction

My mother died when I was seven years old. At a time when most children were concerned with nothing more than their play, I was facing questions that I would rather have not faced: What happens when people die? Will I ever feel happy again? What can I do for my family to help them with all of this? Did I do something to bring this about? Why, God, why?

My grandmother died when I was twenty-two. Surely now the questions would be easier to face, I thought. But they were not. Because not only did I have to deal with loss all over again, this loss touched something within me that was still very connected to the loss of my mother, which was connected to other losses, which were somehow connected to God.

My grandfather died when I was twenty-eight. I was, at this point, a priest serving in an active parish, and had been with countless families, offering comfort and solace to those who mourn. Surely I would have more answers this time, I thought. Again, this loss was connected to the losses of my mother and grandmother, which were connected to other losses, which were somehow connected to God.

They're all very complicated, these issues of grief and loss which we all must face. Just when we think we have moved on to a new place, after being stationary in loss's quagmire, something will come up within us that touches it all off again. And, though we thought that all our tears had been shed, though we thought that the aching in our hearts had vanished, the tears and the ache can return, and do return. And with them come the questions: What happens when people die? Will I ever feel happy again? What can I do for my family to help them with all of this? Did I do something to bring this about? Why, God, why?

Although I don't purport to know all the answers, I have begun to discern a very fundamental truth weaving through it all: the best way to understand loss and the grief that comes from it, the best way to begin to comprehend the toll that death can take on the living, is to be aware of the presence of God in our daily lives. If we look for answers elsewhere, our pursuits are worthless.

This book, then, offers reflections for each day of the year. It is my attempt to point out the amazing presence of God in this world, and to offer—if not the answers—at least my attempts at a search for them. Some of the experiences I relate are unique to me—a Benedictine monk and priest—but the truths the experiences relate are as common as humankind. I am absolutely convinced that God is active in our lives in so many ways, and that if we begin to listen for His presence, to see Him in others, to feel Him in our hearts, then the sheer suffering and pain of loss can be transformed in our hearts, and, with God's abundant help, we can begin to truly heal. One day at a time.

JANUARY

"Begin at the beginning ... and go on till you come to the end: then stop."

—Lewis Carroll

I resolve to quit smoking. I resolve to lose weight. I resolve to exercise more. I resolve to eat right. I resolve to relax more. Each year we draw up our list of New Year's resolutions, as if the mere fact that another calendar year is beginning is going to make sure that we are spurred onto action, into growth. And often the list can be laid aside or even forgotten.

There is nothing magical about the first day of January, however, and it is important for us to realize that life itself is a series of an unending patterns of beginnings and endings, beginnings and endings. And somewhere, in between all of these beginnings and endings, we live. And, hopefully, in living, we find grace. And in finding grace we find the courage and strength to begin again.

"Little children, let us love in deed and in truth and not merely talk about it."

—1 John 3:18

There comes a time when we have to put our money where our mouth is. There comes a time when we move from *talking* about love—of what it means, of how it touches us, of how wonderful it is—to *doing* something to make love more present, more real. And, harsh as it may sound, if we expect others to show us love, to help us through rough times, then we need to show that same love to others, even when we feel there is very little we can give, very little we can do. For how will the people in our lives know how to love us—to show us love—if we do not show them?

"Keep thou my feet: I do not ask to see / The distant scene; one step enough for me."

— John Henry Cardinal Newman

If only we could see the future, we might think, how much easier life would be. When we wonder how we will get through something, what a comfort it would be to be able to see just how we will get through it, and when. When we wonder if things will ever be better, how nice it would be to see that they will, and when.

Of course, we cannot know; only God knows. And God doesn't ordinarily let us know what will happen in the future, but He does promise to guide our steps. If we concentrate on those steps, and where they lead us right now, then we can be sure that we will not be led into anything that is beyond our ability to handle it. One step at a time.

4

"*Do what you can, with what you have, where you are.*"

—Theodore Roosevelt

My sister Kathy and I, extroverts, like to talk about our mother as much as we can. We want to talk about everything—what she was like, whether she could sing, how she struggled when truly in pain, what really made her angry, what music she liked—everything. My brother David, more of an introvert, seems to prefer to keep his memories in his own heart where he can best deal with them in his own way. To expect my sister or me to pipe down, or my brother to start launching into soliloquies on the subject is to turn a blind eye to the fact that we all need to work through, not just grief, but life itself, with the personality and quirks and interesting attributes that we've been given.

"You can depend on this: If we have died with him we shall also live with him; If we hold out to the end, we shall reign with him."

—2 Timothy 2:11-12

If only dying with Him and holding out to the end was easier, this business of reigning with Him might appear a little more attractive than it does at first glance. But we know that death—either the daily dying to self that Christians are expected to undergo, or the real physical death that our loved ones have experienced—is far from easy. It makes stringent demands upon us, causes us to suffer and to question. And what about holding out, endurance? How difficult it is to stick with it all, when at our lowest times it can seem like folly, a waste.

6

> "*Of all the things that wisdom provides to make life entirely happy, much the greatest is the possession of friendship.*"

—Epicurus

The phone call telling me of my grandfather's death came and I slumped by the side of the bed, anguished and frightened. I could not—indeed I did not even *want* to—imagine a world in which Gramps didn't exist to tell me stories and fix things for me and make me feel a part of something. I immediately reached for that same phone, and I called my friend Godfrey, because I knew that just because I couldn't imagine something at that moment didn't mean that things couldn't look different when viewed in the light of friendship. And I made a resolution to never block out that light from my life.

"The art of living is more like wrestling than dancing."

—Marcus Aurelius

When we are young we seem to think that life should be one joy after another, and that we should glide through it all blissfully, turning and twirling with delight at the sheer wonder and adventure of it all. As we grow older, and cynicism can take over, we might think of life more in terms of a battle, with constant skirmishes that require our strength and attention to fully take on.

It seems to me the healthiest stance is somewhere in between. Because there are indeed battles in life that can drain us of our energy, and wound us. But, once the battle is over, perhaps the best thing to do is cast off our armor, and dance for joy that the battle didn't kill us, and somehow, was worth the fight.

"There is nothing so strong as gentle-ness, and nothing so gentle as real strength."

— Saint Francis de Sales

Once as a very young boy, my Gramps gave into my whining and agreed to let me hammer a nail into a board on which he was working. Wanting to impress him with the sheer power of my 6-year-old muscles, I swung that hammer with all the might that was in my small body. And I missed the nail. And I swung again and again. And I missed again and again. Gramps finally took the hammer out of my hand, and with half the force that I had been attempting, tapped the nail securely in place. An important lesson for a young boy to learn: sometimes the small, quiet ways of dealing with a situation are exactly the ways that are going to insure something gets done.

"You make the grass grow for the cattle and the plants to serve man's needs."
— Psalm 103:14

When I was a young boy, I was fascinated by gardens. A garden was for me a magical, wondrous place. After my mother died, nothing in my world seemed to be normal or uniform except gardens, offering their testimony that there was order in the world; that, even if through my eyes the world often looked confusing, sad, or chaotic, it clearly was not. It was a world where seeds were laid quite precisely in a row; where each thing had its place; where loving hands tucked the seeds into the bed of the earth, just like a mother. And then, as I saw new life make its way to the top of the soil, I thought how amazing that something as frail as a plant could have the strength to push aside so much soil and appear in our world. How wondrous it was when the plants grew to full size, and I could stand among the corn and be completely hidden from a world that still confused me.

10

"Truly, truly, I say to you, unless a grain of wheat falls into the earth and dies, it remains alone; but if it dies, it bears much fruit."

—John 12:24

Of course, from my vantage point on this side of the earth I never saw what happened to the seed. I never reflected on the dark, cold indifference of the earth. It never dawned on me that the hard exterior of the shell had to crack open and give way to the life that was inside. Mesmerized by the new life present, enticed to hide myself in their shelter as the plants grew, I never knew at what cost all of this occurred. Perhaps if, as a small child, I had known the violent reality of the seed, then the garden wouldn't have seemed so wondrous, so magical. I know now, of course, that it is precisely *because* of the violent reality of the seed that the plant emerges triumphant, beautiful. It is not in spite of the traumas of the dark, cold soil that beauty emerges, but *because* of it.

> *"Human excellence means nothing unless it works with the consent of God."*
>
> —Euripides

Fire. The wheel. Iron tools. The printing press. The steam engine. The telephone. The computer. The history of the human race is marked with amazing accomplishments by its members. When we put our minds to it, we are quite resourceful indeed.

The problem comes when we expect to invent and fix ourselves as easily as we invent and fix objects—we just can't. We need to realize that God is the true inventor, and if we have difficulty getting through things in this life we have to be content with the fact that God is the one that will make things new in us—but on God's time, not necessarily on ours. It is a little lesson in humility for us, because ultimately we are forced to recognize that we are not always the creator, but rather a work ourselves, still very much in progress.

"Call on me in the day of distress."

—Psalm 49

I have heard people say that they don't want to ask God for something, because it seems the only time they turn to Him is when they need something, and they don't want to be hypocritical— needing Him when times are down but not when good things are happening. And whereas prayers of thanksgiving clearly should be a part of our life, if we forget on occasion to tell God thanks, it does not mean that we shouldn't continue to cry out to Him when we are in need. The Lord longs to be a part of our lives, however that may manifest itself. He longs to comfort us in our sorrows, soothe our pain, be with us so we are never alone. Let us never hesitate to call on Him for any reason. For if we do cry out to Him in distress, it just might be that we will soon have something to thank Him for.

> *"The cause of Freedom is the cause of God!"*
>
> —William Lisle Bowles

They were in bondage, the people of Israel. Deprived of liberty, shackled to the harsh realities of a life beyond their control, they cried out to their God, "Deliver us!" And God sent them Moses, himself born of slaves, because He heard their cry, He wanted His people to know blessed freedom. And they did.

They were in bondage, the descendants of Moses, our ancestors. Though God had once freed them, they chose bondage over that freedom, turning away from His liberation and clinging to captivity instead. "Free your people," they cried out. And God sent His Son, born of a woman, because He heard their cry. He wanted His people to know blessed freedom. And they—we—do.

When we find ourselves imprisoned in any way, we must realize that God desires us to be free. And so, we must cry out to Him, and we will be free.

14

> "Clergymen and people who use
> phrases without wisdom sometimes talk
> of suffering as a mystery. It is really a
> revelation."
>
> —Oscar Wilde

"Why?" I would cry in sorrow as a young boy, confused by a world where children could be motherless. "Why?" I still cry as a young man, confused by a world where senseless brutality can seem to surround us at times. And the world spins silently on its perch, and no answer is given me except the answer of the Cross, in whose shadow the world is cast. It is the answer to all of the exasperated "why's" ever uttered. In its silence we learn, not only about the world, but about our very souls.

"Everything you can imagine is real."
—Pablo Picasso

Picasso's genius stemmed from seeing the world and its inhabitants in ways that no one else had ever thought of. He imagined a world where the soft ambiguity of the human form and soft impressions of nature were transformed into stern geometric shapes and vibrant colors, thus inviting people to reflect on the wonders of humanity and the world in new ways. Such was the amazing power of his imagination.

Human beings by nature are imaginative people, and it is often a solace to rely on that imagination. Even if we live in a world of selfish, brutal reality, it is good for us to imagine a world of selfless beauty and love. So too, if we live with the struggles and sadness of loss, we need to imagine a time when the pain will be lessened, the sadness not as gripping. Then we can begin to make the transition from a life imagined to a life lived.

"*This great confidence in God is ours, through Christ.*"

—2 Corinthians 3:4

One of the virtues for which people are constantly searching is more confidence. We need only turn on our television sets late at night to see a toothy man, telling us how we can take charge of our lives and be confident in our abilities, our business transactions, and our relationships. All of this for three easy installments of $49.99!

I think all of these people who are offering their versions of confidence miss the boat. We must first and foremost work on our faith life, and having confidence in God's mercy, God's redeeming love, God's place in our lives and in the lives of others. If we can be confident of this, then we may begin to find that our abilities, our business transactions, our relationships, indeed our very lives, will begin to be viewed in a new light—one of the confidence that can only come from Christ.

"*Yet, though I stooped to feed my children, they did not know that I was their healer.*"

—Hosea 11:3

Most of us know what it means to be healed in one fashion or another. For some of us it is the relief of getting over a cold that we thought would never go away. For some of us it is the blessed relief of a successful surgery and recovery. For some of us it is the peace of mind of being forgiven. Whatever the case, we are nourished by moments of healing; like mother's milk they strengthen us, allow us to survive and grow.

It does us good to recognize that every moment of healing in our lives is of God, who, like a mother, loves us, and stoops down to offer us nourishment. If we are in need of healing of any kind, let us never fail to reach to Him.

18

"Great thoughts come from the heart."
—Marquis de Vauvenargues

One day a few years ago I was looking out the window of my office and I saw a mother walking her third-grade son to the school corner, sending him off with a hug. I was suddenly overcome with sadness, acutely aware of my own third-grade year in which no mother was there to fulfill this important task. How ridiculous, I thought at first; I am an adult, and it was years ago, it doesn't make sense that I should be so affected so many years later. But then I realized that I was thinking with my mind, a mind that says that everything should be fine now. Instead I needed to think with my heart, that said that that moment of sadness somehow—although I didn't understand it then—was a gift.

> *"Life seems to me like a Japanese picture which our imagination does not allow to end in the margin."*
>
> —Oliver Wendell Holmes, Jr.

Most of us are raised on the notion of heaven, that people go to a place of beauty and serenity when they die. And the reality of heaven is a wonderful thing: it helps soothe the pain of loss and offers hope to us who still toil on the earth as well.

So whereas John Lennon encouraged people to imagine there's no heaven, I would encourage just the opposite. The mysteries of life and love cannot be limited to time and space, and if the beautiful colors of our memories of loved ones, and their memories of us, somehow spill out over the margins of our finite lives, then so be it. It gives us a glimpse here on earth of the beautiful portrait of eternity.

"He asked me: Son of man, can these bones come to life?"

—Ezekiel 37:3

How amazing: bare bones slowly developing sinews; flesh appearing; and then, emboldened by the very breath of God the bones begin to spring to life, dancing the ecstatic jig of those given life by God. Where once there was nothing but dust and death, with God life springs forth. How amazing.

He seeks to come to us as well. Our own bones, made stiff from sorrow, dried up from grief, can be given new life if we but allow that same breath to blow over us, through us. But in order to allow the stagnancy of their inertia to be changed into the dance of all things possible, we must desire to change, to grow closer to the one who calls our tired bones to the dance. But if we can receive the grace to change, what an amazing dance it can be, one that can carry us all the way to eternity.

"From the rising of the sun to its setting praised be the name of the Lord."

—Psalm 112

The other morning, in the midst of one of those bad/sad/angry/bewildered moods that can strike us all at any time, I was walking though our living room at about 6:30 in the morning. The autumn sun was just beginning to rise over the valley below, and the colors that were beginning to appear over the misty horizon were breathtaking to behold. I stopped and marveled at the mastery of it all, and realized that the Painter was doing it all for me, wanting me to share in the beauty. That a million other eyes could behold a sunrise didn't seem to matter; at that moment, in that place, it was clearly done just for me. And I needed it.

"*Yesternight the sun went hence, /
And yet is here today.*"

—John Donne

The next morning, after darkness had
once again reclaimed the earth, I
went to stand at that east-facing window, needing to experience once again
the blessed promise that the sun's rays
seems to be able to paint upon my very
soul. And standing there, receiving my
sun, was Brother Robert, staring at the
portrait that was unfolding before him.
How dare him, I thought at first; that
sun was made for me. But then a calm
came over me, as I realized that, just as I
had needed to be healed by beauty, perhaps he too needed the same thing. And
God provided for him as he did for me.

"After the earthquake there was a fire—but the Lord was not in the fire. After the fire there was a tiny whispering sound."

—1 Kings 19:12

What an awe-inspiring, if not frightening, prospect Elijah was faced with. Go to the mouth of the cave, God told him, and I will pass by. And the wind roared, rocks were crushed, the earth quaked and the air around him burst into flames—much of the theatrics one would expect from an all-powerful God. And yet, God was in none of that. No, He seemed to be saying to Elijah, if you want to feel My presence, if you want to know that I am here with you, look not to dramatics and sound effects, listen to the small whispering voice within you.

He says the same to us. And we realize that if God can enter into the quiet secret places of our hearts, then He most certainly can touch anything that is already there. What an awe-inspiring, if not frightening, prospect.

"Thus happiness depends, as Nature shows, / Less on exterior things than most suppose."

—William Cowper

"If only I would win the lottery," people say and then go on to list the things that they would procure that would definitely make their lives better. Swimming pools, cars, better homes, vacations—all of these things would so crowd life with a new-found happiness that there would be little room for anything else, most of all sorrow.

It's hard to convince people that the true key to happiness lies in a heart open to what the Lord desires. And that the Lord may desire other things for us than possessions is a fact quite often ignored by people.

"Under his wings you will find refuge."

—Psalm 90

"He always put this umbrella up for me when the sun got too bad," a recently widowed woman lamented to me one day when I was sitting with her on her patio, her shaky hands shielding her eyes from the afternoon glare. I quickly jumped up and did just that, realizing as I did it that she wasn't simply lamenting sun in her eyes, but a sense of security, of being taken care of, that death had stripped her of. And so I started telling stories of God who cared so passionately and intimately for us, who longed to shelter us in the wings of love. And, in very different words, she told me stories of the same love and care, as the sun crept below the grain elevator on the horizon.

"Where there is sorrow there is holy ground."

—Oscar Wilde

Perhaps the most jarring part of a monastic funeral is at the cemetery, when the abbot throws a shovel full of dirt on the coffin, already having been placed in the earth. Visitors inevitably jump as the sound echoes through the pine trees that line the cemetery, as if an earthquake has disturbed the quiet peacefulness of the gathering. Thud. It is the sound of hearts breaking. Thud. It is the sound of voiceless crying. Thud. It is the sound of pain, of loss.

It is undeniable, however, that it is also the sound of something sacred, for that thud is a testimony not only to the reality and finality of loss, but also to the reality and finality of God's love, manifested by the image of a cross standing against the blood red sky, while the earth quaked in reverence.

"Let me now sing of my friend, my friend's song concerning his vineyard."
—Isaiah 5:1

In the afternoon haze of the courts of Jerusalem, they heard his voice. Who was the prophet, this Isaiah, who spoke to them? Intrigued, they gathered closer to listen. He spoke to them of a beautiful vineyard on a hillside, and with the power of his words painted pictures in their minds so intense and detailed that the finest of painters could not begin to capture them. And so they listened, transfixed on the brush strokes that were his words and images. But then something happened. In the midst of his amazing words, the picture suddenly became too clear. These wild grapes were they, themselves. Isaiah had gone from being a beautiful artist to a prophet, painting a far more realistic picture than anyone wanted to see. His final message: God wants you to change your lives. And no one likes to change.

"For this reason, I tell you, the kingdom of God will be taken away from you and given to a people that will yield a rich harvest."

—Matthew 21: 43

In the cool of the evening, in the temple precincts of Jerusalem, they heard His voice. Who was this Jesus who spoke to them? He spoke to them of a vineyard as well, but spiced his story up with tales of treachery and intrigue, and eventually, murder. And so they listened, absorbing his words as if they were a beautiful, dramatic piece of music. But then, something happened. The composer of this symphony changed keys abruptly. These people, the ones who killed the very son of the vineyard owner, that was this group of listeners. His final message: God wants you to change your lives. And so, challenged to change, the people turned their backs on Him and His beautiful words, because we all know that we need to change to grow and move on, but it can sometimes be so painful.

"All is change; all yields its place and goes."

—Euripides

There can be a real comfort in grief, oddly enough. In a world where so much changes, where people are born and die every day, there can be a strange comfort indeed in merely sticking with that grief which always remains. It's my suffering, we seem to say; at least I can count on it.

But to truly grow, to truly allow life to triumph over death, we must pick ourselves up and move on. The pain, the sorrow, the regret—all of these remain somehow a part of us, but they are transformed into avenues of possibility, of hope. Isaiah and the prophets, Jesus Christ—they were all right: God wants us to change our lives. And though this change, this moving on, is painful, we can always turn to their words and examples to help show us the way.

30

"*Lord for your faithful people, life has changed, not ended.*"

—from the Preface of the
Rite of Christian Burial

At the visitation for my mother, my father, in what had to be one of the most difficult tasks of his life, approached the casket of his wife, holding the hand of his seven- year-old son, laying that hand on hers, ever the teacher, to show the truth of the body being a vessel for the spirit.

My senses exploded: the sight of my mother, the cold hard feeling of her hand, the overpowering smell of the flowers, the soft music playing in the background, the taste of my tears running into the corner of my mouth. With all of this came a sense of hyper-reality—it was all too real, a bit exaggerated. And yet, I also knew at that moment, that as real as this death was, life was a grander reality. Such epiphanies can help make sense of things, even to a child.

"The hope set before us ... is like an anchor for our lives, an anchor safe and sure."

—Hebrews 6:19

One of the most moving parts of the National Holocaust Memorial and Museum in Washington, DC is an exhibit called Daniel's Story, which tells the story of the Holocaust through the eyes of one child. The tone of the exhibit is amazing. No matter what unspeakable tragedies surround Daniel, no matter what he is forced to endure, in every word he utters one can sense, through the darkness of his world, the unmistakable light of hope. And that this hope comes from one so young can only speak of the reality that hope is not something we acquire, but it is something deep within us, innate.

"I've lost hope," we've all felt from time to time, and perhaps rightly so. But we need to remember that if we've *lost* it, we can *find* it again, for its light is always with us.

FEBRUARY

"You must sit down, says Love, and taste my meat: So I did sit and eat."
—George Herbert

Guilt surrounding the pain of loss can often be the most severe. We can be plagued by unkind words or actions that we directed at loved ones who are no longer with us, and their silence seems to indict us. We can have difficulty letting go of hurts that we may have experienced at their hands as well, and we long to tell them how much they have hurt us, feeling bad at the same time for thinking ill of the dead.

We must be confident that Love— the love that can bring forth a baby from the womb of a virgin, the love that can cause the deaf to hear, the blind to see, and the lame to leap like stags, the love that can bring life forth where there had only before been death—this Love can so fill us that the hunger of guilt and remorse can be vanquished, if we but taste of its promise.

2

"The march of the human mind is slow."

—Edmund Burke

There are times when we can look back at our lives and see the hand of God—in the people we've encountered, in the struggles we've endured, in the joys we've celebrated. And at those times we can just begin, perhaps, to wrap our minds around the notion of God's plan, of life in the image of Christ. It can, at times, make sense to us.

And then, something can happen (usually something bad) and our minds, our hearts can be hurled back into confusion. I don't *get* it, God. How is this supposed to help me? Why did this have to happen? And in moments like these it can be as if the insight of which we were once so sure is gone, replaced in our minds by doubt, confusion.

Our minds can be attuned to God once again, we must understand; it just takes some time.

"Your heavenly Father knows all that you need."

—Matthew 6:32

People spend a great deal of time worrying about all kinds of things. There can be worthwhile worries: Will I make enough money to support my family? Will I have enough to eat? Will I be able to do with my life what I feel I should? Will I be able to move on with my life after this tragedy? And there are worries that are less than pressing: What will I wear to the party? What if I don't get the promotion? Will I be able to afford that new sports car?

As life is filled with all kinds of worries, it is important to be able to distinguish between those really important questions, and those questions that really are not all that significant. And the answer to all of the really pressing questions of life, the destination of all our searches, is God—plain and simple. And often we'll find He's usually answered the question before we even ask it, if we pay attention.

4

"Sometimes, when one person is missing, the whole world seems depopulated."
—Lamartine

When the bells began to toll announcing the death of Father Theodore, I felt cheated. He had been working in South Dakota for some time, and I hadn't seen him in years. "I never got to say goodbye," I lamented over and over again, his absence suddenly becoming more acute because of its finality.

But since then, every time I laugh at an outrageous story about him, every time my lips curl into a smile at the mere thought of him, and, every time, in the midst of the laughter and the smiles I sense the familiar pang of loss, I realize I *am* saying goodbye. It's just that goodbyes take time.

"In a word, you must be perfected as your heavenly Father is perfect."

—Matthew 5:48

I've heard this passage translated as "you must be perfect" and I have to admit I like adding that "ed" onto the end of it. Who among us is perfect? Who among us can even hope to strive for real perfection? No one, of course, for the limits of our humanity are all too real.

But we can hope to be perfected. We can hope that graces we receive in life will strengthen us, draw us closer to that perfection which the Father possesses in its fullness. But if we truly desire to be perfected, then we must see all that life has to offer as grace, as a possible means to that perfected-ness. *All* that life has to offer, not just what we like. This is difficult to do, because, after all, no one is perfect.

"Learn a lesson from the way the wildflowers grow. They do not work; they do not spin. Yet I assure you, not even Solomon in all his splendor was arrayed like one of these."

—Matthew 6:28-29

Recently I asked a group of junior-high students what they most wanted out of life. The list was astounding in its detail and a bit disheartening in its content: cars, homes, stereos, in-home theatre systems, and—of course—high-paying jobs that would insure all of this *stuff*. I was about to preach to them about what really matters in life when I noticed one of them eyeing my new pair of shoes. We all know that money (and the things it can bring us) won't buy us happiness; but all too often (especially when sadness hits) I think we all try to *rent* it a bit, shutting out the recognition that the true stuff of happiness (time, support, love) can be purchased at no cost whatsoever.

"All the ends of the earth have seen the salvation of our God."

—Psalm 97

To get from the monastery to my office, I have to walk through our church—something I do numerous times each day. At every trek through the church, I take a moment to bow at the altar, the symbol of Christ in the church, but I rarely notice anything else. I don't pay attention to the beautiful marble floors, the soaring Romanesque arches, the magnificent stained glass windows. Such amazing brilliance is all around me but, because of eyes made dull by routine, I hardly ever notice it.

The entire world has seen the salvation and glory of God and, all too often, because of eyes made dull by routine, by stress, by suffering, by pain, we hardly ever notice it. Just because we fail to notice it, though, doesn't mean it's not there.

7

F
E
B
R
U
A
R
Y

8

"All men who live with any degree of serenity live by some assurance of grace."

—Reinhold Niebuhr

When a monk is dying, the rest of us take turns sitting with him, so that he will not die alone. And so it was my turn to sit with Brother Casimir in what ended up being the last morning of his life here on earth. At first the heat of the room, the drone of the oxygen machine, the antiseptic smell, and the labored breathing all combined to fill the room, making me feel crowded, claustro-phobic. But the longer I sat there, uncomfortable, I began to realize that even more than all of this crowding the room (and specifically *because* of all that filled the room) grace was powerfully present as well. We can try to crowd it out of our lives, but it just won't go away.

"Jesus was led into the desert by the Spirit to be tempted by the devil."

—Matthew 4:1

He could have given in, and things might have gone better for him. If Jesus would have turned stones into bread, thrown Himself from the highest point in the temple, and taken command of all the kingdoms of the earth, surely more people would have believed in Him, more people would have acknowledged Him as God. And this Kingdom of God that He kept preaching about would have been realized right then and there, instead of everyone waiting for its fulfillment like we still do today. Yes, I suppose, He could have given in, but He didn't. Because, you see, to give in would have meant that Jesus was buying into what the world thought He should be, and He was, instead, about his Father's business, a business that—much to the confusion and consternation of the world—said that life could actually come from death.

10

"Every charitable act is a stepping stone toward heaven."

—Henry Ward Beecher

My sophomore year in college my classmates and I were conscripted to volunteer for supper service at St. John's Bread Line. We were positively glowing with that good feeling that one can get when one feels really useful, genuinely needed. How wonderful we felt to be putting our faith into action.

The more we worked there, however, (and very hard work it ended up being) the distinction between the ministers and the ones being ministered to became blurred. We soon became powerfully aware that these holy and righteous acts of ours (which we imagined were inching us closer to heaven) were indeed opportunities to share in the wonders of humanity—good and ill—and thus see a little bit of heaven here on earth.

"He approached the elder [son] and said, 'Son, go out and work in the vineyard today.' The son replied, 'I am on my way, sir;' but he never went."

—Matthew 21:28

Maybe his intentions were good, that first son. Mindful of his duties, obedient to his father, maybe he really did intend to go to the vineyard and work. "I am on my way, sir." But, who knows, a lot of things can happen on the way to the vineyard. Maybe there were people in the vineyard he just didn't want to see. Maybe he didn't want to risk being stung by the bees that surrounded the sweet excess of the fruit. Maybe he began to think about how hard he had worked in the vineyard the last time he was there, and decided that he was too tired. Maybe his intentions were good, but, who knows, a lot can happen on the way to the vineyard.

12

"Then the man came to his second son and said the same thing. This son said in reply, 'No I will not;' but afterward he regretted it and went."

—Matthew 21:29-30

Maybe his intentions weren't so good, this second son. Work in the vineyard? "No, I will not." Maybe he didn't need temptation to present itself to him like his brother did; maybe he already knew that there was a pretty fun world outside of the drudgery of that vineyard, and he wanted to be a part of it all. And it could be that he had no intention whatsoever of working in that vineyard, thinking instead of the great possibilities that existed for him. Maybe his intentions weren't so good, but then again maybe he knew all along in the back of his mind that the vineyard was where he belonged, and just maybe after his, "No, I will not," he headed in that direction anyway. Who knows? A lot can happen on the way to the vineyard.

"And they shall plant vineyards and eat the fruit of them."

—Isaiah 65:21

All too often, especially when we are enjoying periods of prosperity and serenity, we can make ourselves believe that life should be this prosperous and serene all of the time. But the fact of the matter remains that, even though life can be delicious and sweet indeed, it takes effort and action to help make it that way. Living, grieving, learning, growing, loving—all of these elements of life's vineyard need tending to. And there will be times when we fear the exhaustion, the stings that can be a part of it all. Even though we may fear these things, we need to be resolute in our desire for the kingdom, because not only is the fruit worth the toil, but the trip there can be pretty amazing as well. Because a lot can happen on the way to the vineyard.

14

"Jesus said to his disciples: 'Peace is my farewell to you, my peace is my gift to you.'"

—John 14:27

Elsewhere He spoke of a peace where the closest family members would be divided against each other, and it begs the question, "Do we really want His peace?" If this is what His gift of peace means, then perhaps our tendency is to wish to return the gift, exchanging it for something that is less taxing on us. The world is filled with enough division and sorrow as it is; why go looking for more?

The Lord's notion of peace is much deeper than just a nice calmness in our lives, a lack of friction. His peace is that which makes us aware that no matter what, He will not abandon us, He will not leave us to struggle in this world alone, even in the face of the sorrow that can come about in our lives as a result of our following Him in this mysterious way of peace. It's a strange gift, this peace, but in the end it is the most precious we could hope for.

"The soul is healed by being with children."

—Fyodor Dostoevsky

After the funeral of my Uncle Billy, our family gathered at my cousin Diane's house for the obligatory post-funeral food fest. The mood, understandably, was somber. Adults sat around in clutches, passing the time of day, but not really *talking*, as adults are often wont to do. Every sad, exaggerated pause was avoided by a phrase such as, "This potato salad is the best! What's your secret?" All of a sudden, in the midst of it all, my niece Abigail burst noisily into the room, her cheeks flushed with the excitement of her latest game. "Abby!" her mother reprimanded as the other parents looked on with knowing glances. I set aside my fried chicken and green bean casserole and followed the little piper out of the room, certain she was on to something.

"Everyone should carefully observe which way his heart draws him, and then choose that way with all his strength."

—Hasidic saying

I was in a park in downtown St. Louis one day, on a break from a conference I was attending, and I encountered a truly wonderful sight. Standing in the middle of one of the fountain pools there, looking up to the heavens with a beatific smile, heartily enjoying a bratwurst dripping with mustard, was a man in a very formal business suit, socks and shoes removed and pants rolled up to his knees. "That man obviously has problems," the woman standing next to me said, observing the curious scene, and she was probably right. But the more I reflected on it, was touched by the sheer joy that obviously was bursting forth from his heart, I began to think that he quite possibly had the solutions as well.

"And he breathed on them and said: 'Receive the Holy Spirit.'"

—John 20:22

Though fear is human, the overcoming of it is divine, for Jesus Himself stood in the midst of frightened human beings, and all the fearful thoughts were replaced by thoughts of praise and awe: He had indeed risen, as He said He would. And even if they had plenty of good reasons to fear, Jesus put their confusing lives into perspective: "Peace be with you," He said, and then He breathed on them, the cool wonder of His breath overtaking them and quenching the heat of the fear that was so oppressively present in that room. When we suffer one loss in our lives, it is understandable to fear another. But the same promise of peace and the Spirit that tempered the fear of the early disciples can temper our fear as well, and replace its uncomfortable heat with a refreshing breath, with the coolness of an empty tomb.

"And he was transfigured before them, and his face shone like the sun, and his garments became white as light."

—Matthew 17:2

The days are getting longer. Each morning when I wake up, I notice more and more light in the sky, more streaks of color in the east. The light cheers me and warms my heart. Daily I am able to be surrounded more by its wonder, its warmth, its promise, its hope. I think that is the most compelling aspect of the light—it can be a vessel of such hope. Even at times when so much darkness can fill our lives, bringing with it the appearance of an unending night, the light comes, blinding in its hope, radiant in its promise. That same light, that same promise, that same hope is extended to us as well. If we truly hope in God, if we trust His promises to us, then no matter how much darkness reigns in our lives, no matter how often we view our world through the dreary shades of night, we, too can be transfigured.

"Anyone who hears my words and puts them into practice is like the wise man who built his house on rock."

—Matthew 7:24

Sometimes we can put our trust in possessions: if only I had this or that I would be able to shake the emptiness and sadness that seems to so frequently crowd my life. Sometimes we can put our trust in other people: all I need is to have a better relationship with (you fill in the blank) and my problems would go away. Sometimes we can put our trust in work: if I just reach the next level of my job, I will be able to relax and really enjoy life. Sometimes we put our trust in the Lord: if only I can grow closer to Jesus, my life will make more sense.

We don't need a book to tell us which of these things are solid foundations, and which aren't. But if we do need a book, I suggest the Bible.

"Is anything too marvelous for the Lord to do?"

—Genesis 18:14

The giggle gave her away. Sarah, quite old and well past childbearing years, overheard three mysterious strangers tell her old husband Abraham that by that time next year she would have a son. How preposterous a notion, and so Sarah, eyes rolling, head shaking, laughed at the absurdity of it all, and the Lord heard her giggle.

He had the last laugh, of course, because a year later, when Abraham was 100 years old and Sarah somewhere near that, little Isaac had come onto the scene.

The moral: Never underestimate just how far our absurd God will go to show His love for us. He'll always have the last laugh.

"We are astonished at thought, but sensation is equally wonderful."

—Voltaire

My sister has started wearing the same perfume that my Aunt Katie wore when I was a child. I haven't seen Aunt Katie in years, but one hug from my sister and it all comes back to me: lying on the couch in her house, wrapped in an orange and black afghan, her poodle Mitzie resting near me. They happen every now and then, these "scentories": I smell cinnamon and suddenly I'm sitting at the counter, watching Grandma make her famous rolls; I smell leather and I'm sitting on my Grandpa Lewis' lap in his big old chair; I smell leaves burning and I'm playing in the leaves while my mother watches from a lawn chair. For a moment, they're all here with me again, and, though it makes me sad, I can't deny that there is joy there as well. And I breathe it in.

"Look towards him and be radiant."

—Psalm 33

John Fisher, we are told, recited this line right before he was martyred. It seems he was able to see the rays of the sun peeking over the shape of the gallows that would soon hold his body, and he saw in that sun the true Light of the World, the Light that he had every confidence would snatch him from the darkness of death.

Such inspiration is not uncommon on the lips of martyrs. And that which has enabled countless people over the centuries to view death as an avenue to something greater is deep within our hearts as well. We need to call upon our radiant God to help us find it, even when we face life's little martyrdoms at an alarming rate.

"For in the dew of little things the heart finds its morning and is refreshed."

—Kahlil Gibran

"Watch this!" four-year-old Abigail shouted excitedly as she prepared to mount her bicycle without training wheels for the first time. And down the sidewalk she rode shakily, an enormous smile spilling out all over her cherubic face, while we all cheered wildly. Car after car drove by in the street, and not one driver seemed to pay the scene any mind, doubtless involved in their own thoughts, brows furrowed with more serious matters. And those of us present for Abigail's triumph knew that it wasn't an earth-shattering event of global importance. But at the time it seemed pretty close.

"But Lot's wife looked back, and she was turned into a pillar of salt."

—Genesis 26

She has become the poster-child of regret. Frozen, for all time, her lips beginning to trace the words, "What if," she stands as a symbol for all of us who have wondered, from time to time, if we said the right thing, did the right thing. Maybe she worried that there were those in her doomed city who would perish before she had a chance to tell them how important they were to her, or perhaps offer apologies. Who knows what she was thinking as the taste of regret turned salty upon her lips.

We can learn two important lessons from this woman. First of all, we need learn that regret rarely allows us to move forward, but instead can freeze us in attitudes of hurt and pain. And secondly, Lot's wife teaches us that we should be extra vigilant in living our lives in such a manner that regret is not a part of them.

"Blessed are the poor in spirit, for theirs is the kingdom of heaven."

—Matthew 5:3

"Be strong, he would have wanted it that way." "That which doesn't kill us only makes us stronger." In times of sorrow we can readily give into the notion that we always have to be strong, we always have to have our act together, we always have to know all the answers. And from this storehouse of strength, somehow we can move on, can function, can do all the things we need to do.

In opposition to this is the idea of Jesus that those who aren't always strong, those who struggle and wonder, those whose souls know the sheer emptiness and poverty of loss—somehow, these are the ones who are strong, are blessed. Perhaps what we perceive of as strength isn't really strength after all.

"Blessed are those who mourn, they shall be comforted."

—Matthew 5:4

In all of sacred scripture there are perhaps no other words as courageous in their simplistic optimism than these. How, we might venture to ask, are the mourners to be comforted? Jesus doesn't answer; He simply moves on to the next Beatitude, leaving the question hanging in the air like a fog, affecting our vision, our sense of normalcy.

But the answer is there—perhaps not as concretely as we would like—but it is there nonetheless. Because who among us has not mourned? Who among us has not felt the depths of our heart pierced with sadness? And that which has allowed humanity to keep moving in spite of the pain for millennia—call it what you will—is what will somehow allow us to keep moving, bringing us to the realization that we are indeed blessed.

"Blessed are the meek, for they shall inherit the earth."

—Matthew 5:5

It's a little hard to swallow sometimes, this notion of the meek inheriting the earth. One can look around and see powerful, corrupt tycoons and rulers of peoples quite literally taking what they want, while many others suffer and go without, leading lives of quiet desperation. The meek get trampled, while those strong and wise in the world seem to be doing most of the inheriting.

But in the quiet simplicity of meek hearts can rest something so powerful that the leaders of this world are powerless in comparison. And that is love, pure and simple. Love which can turn hearts of stone into hearts of flesh. Love which can give seekers their ultimate destination. Love which even death cannot destroy. If we look around and see people who meekly live their lives in accordance with this love, we'll find that the earth is already theirs.

"Blessed are those who hunger and thirst for righteousness, for they shall be satisfied."

—Matthew 5:6

I learned that righteousness means act-ing in accord with God's law, seeking what God seeks, desiring what God desires. And this definition can be a bit hazy at times. How can we know what God's law is, when so many people interpret it in so many ways? How can we know what God seeks, when the searching of so many people leads them in such varying directions? How can we know what God desires, when so many people brandish the words, "It's God's will," like swords, cutting down those who may see God's desires elsewhere? Confusion is understandable.

There is no confusion, however, in this: God loves us passionately. And per-haps what God desires more than any-thing is that we know this love and allow it to shape and mold our lives. Then we shall be satisfied indeed.

MARCH

"Blessed are the merciful, for they shall obtain mercy."

—Matthew 5:7

When I made the decision to volunteer my time at Bonaventure House, a residence for people with AIDS on Chicago's north side, I was amazed at the resistance that I encountered from people, based mainly on ignorance of how the disease was transmitted and the possibility of "catching it" somehow. The most distressing line, though, came from a relative: "Why would you waste your time with those people? They got what they deserved."

A statement such as this belies ignorance of a basic tenet of humanity: we are all connected somehow. The suffering of one person affects the whole group somehow, even if we can't always see that. And if we don't show mercy to all people who share in the wonders of humanity with us, we just may find that we will have a hard time feeling that merciful connection when we need it most.

2

"Blessed are the pure in heart, for they shall see God."

—Matthew 5:8

Not too long after my mother died, I remember my father's mentally-challenged brother coming to stay with us for a while. Whenever sadness would overwhelm me, Uncle Billy would set me on his lap and show me his pocket watch and harmonica, and rub my head. My grief would remain, of course, but its hold on me was significantly tempered, lessened by this simple, beautiful man and his gentle ways.

We sometimes look for great revelations, for instant insights as to why God allows certain things to happen in the world that bring about sadness. More often than not, these questions go unanswered, or at least in the ways that we *want* them answered. But if we look hard enough, in the loving caresses of simple humanity, the extraordinary presence of God is made manifest.

"Blessed are the peacemakers, for they shall see God."

—Matthew 5:9

Regret is one of the most tragic of human emotions. Thoughts such as, "If only I would have," "I should have done ..." and "Why didn't I ever say ..." race through our minds, causing a battle ground between ideals of what should have been and what really happened. And, as in all battles, the wounds encountered can be significant.

But the peace for which we often pray, the peace that makes us blessed, can begin to heal the wounds, even if the scars remain as reminders of the battle. In moving from what should have been to what is, and *accepting* what is, we move out of the way of the barbed arrows of regret to the peaceful balm of acceptance.

"Eat your bread with joy, drink your wine with a merry heart."

—Ecclesiastes 9:7

When I was growing up, the kitchen was the place where visitors were received. Stories told, sorrows shared, gossip exchanged, jokes recounted—it all happened around the kitchen table, usually with a fresh pot of coffee and some rolls at hand. And when I think about it, the kitchen is the perfect place for this activity. Because just as there is something ultimately satisfying about filling our empty stomachs with food and drink, so too there is something wonderful about filling our lives with friendship. Sometimes it can be more needed than food and drink, and ultimately more satisfying as well.

"I have promised, and I will do it, says the Lord."

—Ezekiel 37:14

God said there would be light and there was. God said Adam wouldn't be alone and he wasn't. God said Abraham would be the father of a great nation and he was. God said I will be born into your midst and He was. God said I will teach you what love is all about and He did. God said I will suffer and die that you may live and He did.

So when we find ourselves doubting, when we find that we are angry or bewildered by God's apparent callousness, when we wonder if He really cares at all, it does us good to go over His track record and realize He hasn't failed us yet.

6

"I will never leave you until I have done what I promised you."

—Genesis 28:15

Although we may want to, we can't know all the answers. And, since there are things that we don't know, we need to rely on faith—pure and simple. What if there is nothing after we die? Faith: "He who believes in me shall never die." What if we can't find our way? Faith: "I am the way." What if the sorrow never departs us? Faith: "I will change your mourning into dancing."

The words of the Scriptures, the examples of our fellow Christians throughout the ages, the Tradition of the Church all point to the answers of the questions that can so plague us in life. But in the end, it is Faith that will enable us to see that we are not left alone, and that all of it will be fulfilled. "Lord, increase our faith," is an earnest cry for the answers.

"*Praise God from whom all blessings flow.*"

—Thomas Ken

The words are familiar, and many of us can't read them without hearing an accompanying tune. In this doxology we have an encapsulation of our entire relationship with God: one of gratitude. How often have we heard or even sung these words and not given them much thought? How often has the sword of familiarity cut through the potential to hear these words and recognize in them the amazing truth: absolutely everything we have, everything that sustains us, everything that allows us to live—all of it comes from God.

What a reason to praise God. What a reason to shake off the torpor of familiarity and search for meaning anew.

"Jesus wept."

—John 11:35

I once heard an undoubtedly good-intentioned minister say to a grieving widow, "Too many tears send the message that we doubt the resurrection of the dead." I didn't correct him (he had, after all, been in the ministry before I was even born) but I couldn't help thinking how off track he was. Jesus' mourning of his friend Lazarus gave birth to tears even though he knew for a fact that in a matter of minutes Lazarus would be alive, set free from the darkness of the bonds of the tomb. And so perhaps the tears didn't speak of doubt of the resurrection of the dead, but acknowledgement of the toll it takes on the living.

"Winter is come and gone, but grief returns with the revolving year."

—Percy Bysshe Shelley

After her beloved husband, Albert, died, Queen Victoria followed the custom of the time and began adorning herself in the black of mourning. But when the acceptable time of mourning had come to an end, she nevertheless continued to drape her ample frame in black, as if to say that she would never be finished mourning the one she loved so dearly.

Time may make the pain of loss less sharp, but it cannot be eradicated entirely. And so as one year turns into another, we need to realize that each new season may bring about memories and reflections that are going to make the loss seem present in new ways. Our task then is not to "get over it," somehow, as if it's inappropriate to be feeling what we do; rather our task is to acknowledge the grief, but make sure that we don't allow it to stop us completely.

"Beauty will save the world."

—Fydor Dosteovsky

Being from the Midwest, my first view of the ocean (the Atlantic, to be specific) occurred when I was ten years old. We had been driving in the car for what seemed like years to my young mind, and the scene in the car was typical vacation fare: my brother annoying me by crossing the imaginary line I had drawn in the back seat; me annoying my father with the interminable, "Are we there yet?"; my father annoying my stepmother by not asking for directions when we were clearly lost.

And suddenly, in the midst of all of this, the ocean came into view. The bickering stopped, as we were all struck silent by the majesty of it. It all returned, of course—the annoying, unpleasant realities of life—but for a moment we were able to rise above it all by drinking in the salvific wonder of sheer beauty.

"For in Christ's coach saints sweetly sing / As they to glory ride therein."
—Edward Taylor

Most of us, if asked where we stood on the saint-to-sinner scale, would most likely place ourselves closer to the sinner side, and perhaps rightly so. But the scale is not as broad as we think, and the difference between the two not so grand that Christ could not bridge it with the gap of His out-stretched arms.

And so we can dare to hope that not only can we one day ride to glory, singing with the other saints, but so, too, among that number will be those whom we loved.

"I always do the first line well, but have trouble doing the others."

—Molière

"It was a dark and stormy night," countless authors have begun, only to have the story fall apart in the second paragraph. Even if we don't write ourselves, this phenomenon is not unknown to us. We have the best intentions of beginning something, of knowing what is the best course of action, but for all our good intentions we sometimes have difficulty following through.

Knowing that this is a part of our human condition can help us. Because when we have made our mind up how the story should go, and yet can't seem to follow through with it, we can always go back to the beginning. Bit by bit, with patience in ourselves and others, we begin to have the strength to move on from the first line, to see beyond the dark and stormy night to the bright and clear day that follows.

> "'What sort of man is this,' they said, 'that even the winds and the sea obey him?'"
>
> —Matthew 8:27

The winds assailed, blowing fiercely, chafing skin, quickening hearts, blustering fear. The waters threatened, soaking skin, quickening hearts, saturating fear. And then, in the midst of it all, boat nearly capsized, He stood, and took the sea and winds to task. And the winds and water calmed, skin refreshed, hearts gratefully slowing, fear evaporating. Who is this that can stand in the midst of elements quite beyond our feeble control and take them to task?

It is the same one who can still calm the storms of our own lives, who still has the ability in the midst of a whirlwind to take it all to task—the suffering, the sadness, the doubt, the anguish, the numbness—and say to them, "You will not have the final say here, I will!"

We need only get in the boat with Him.

14

> *"Into each life some rain must fall, /
> some days must be dark and dreary."*
>
> —Longfellow

I had a professor once say that people who wish for great wealth and happiness will never be satisfied, because they'll never be wealthy and happy enough. Who knows if this is really true, but I think there is some wisdom to it, especially on the happiness end. In times of great elation we sometimes find ourselves wondering why life can't be like this all the time, or at least more often. But the reality, of course, is that this sort of unending bliss is just not possible.

And so, when we have our times of inestimable happiness, we need constantly be aware that it is a gift and, most likely, a short-lived one at that. But so too, in our dark days, do we need to be aware that this cannot last forever either, and so accept the rainfall with resignation, while at the same time not fearing to look for the sun.

"I will be like the dew for Israel: he shall blossom like the lily."

—Hosea 14:5

L ilies are a wonderful flower, and it is no surprise that they have become synonymous with the joy of Easter. Their scent is intoxicating; I love to walk into our church Easter morning and breathe in the beauty of the scent of the lilies mingled with incense and candle wax.

Perhaps more amazing than these potted, planned lilies, though, are the surprise lilies that seem to spring from nowhere. Nestled amid trees or in open fields, they spring to earth as a testimony to the surprise of the empty tomb, to the surprise of a God who at any time and in any place, can spring up in our lives, intoxicating us with His beauty.

"This is courage in a man: to bear unflinchingly what heaven sends."

—Euripides

When I was young, I used to love to spend winter Saturday afternoons watching old movies on Channel 11. Ordinarily it was action-packed fare: Errol Flynn as a swashbuckling pilot, James Cagney as a gangster with a heart of gold, Johnny Weismuller swinging on his vines, John Wayne riding high on his horse. I was captivated by these men and the courage they exhibited in fighting off their adversaries. I hoped one day to be as courageous as they, to lead a life filled with such intrigue and excitement.

The older I get, the more I realize that courage bears less a resemblance to these figures than it does to my Gramps, quietly playing solitaire in a kitchen left empty by my Grandma's passing. We needn't look to a pirate's ship or the Old West to see true courage; we need only look to the strength that allows us to move forward in life.

"No doubt my poetry errs on the side of oddness."

—Gerard Manley Hopkins

Some of the people whom history has judged the greatest were, in their own times, quite misunderstood. Jesus was constantly being challenged by the Pharisees about things He said and did that just didn't seem to fit with the prevailing religious thought of the day. How odd. Francis of Assisi stripped himself naked and gave all of his clothes to his father in the town square. How odd. Bernadette of Lourdes kept having conversations with a beautiful woman that no one else seemed to be able to see. How odd.

And so, if others try to make us feel that there is only one way to pray, to grieve, to express ourselves, we need not automatically give in to their way of thinking. God who is infinite can and does help us in ways that are as different as we are different. How odd.

*"Pain is deeper than all thought;
laughter is higher than all pain."*
—Elbert Hubbard

Father Julian has the uncanny ability to make me laugh at the most serious of times—usually when we are in church. We will be listening to a solemn reading of the account of someone's martyrdom, for example; I'll look up across the choir and catch his eye, and the slightest of gestures—a smirk, a raised eyebrow—will for some reason always bring about laughter in me— laughter, of course, that I have to suppress because it is not appropriate to laugh in church.

Or so they say.

I'm not so sure. The world is filled enough with sorrow and tragedy and routine and seriousness. Sometimes laughter is the only thing that can cover all of that, raise low spirits higher. And if raising low spirits higher isn't of God, I don't know what is.

*"Jesus said to his disciples: 'I am send-
ing you out like sheep among wolves.'"*
—Matthew 10:16

It can be a dangerous place, the world.
In addition to the violence, disasters,
and accidents that can season the world
in which we live, so too can be human
misunderstanding, sorrow, division,
enmity. And it can be a natural response,
at times, to want to flee the world, to
remove ourselves from those things
which seem to take their toll on us. But it
is specifically into the world—and all that
it holds for us—that the Lord sends us. It
is specifically in the world that, even
though we may encounter grief and loss
and suffering, we will also encounter the
grace to overcome it. Such is the promise
of the Good Shepherd, who won't let the
wolves of the world overtake us, His
sheep.

"Come, gentle Spring! ethereal mild-ness, come."

—James Thomson

The winter can become a habit, a strange solace in and of itself. Wrapped against the blistering breezes, shut away from the ice and snow, steeled against the darkness of its night we can become so accustomed to the season's battles that we look not for the spring's relief. If nothing else, we can at least count on the harshness of winter, which offers few surprises.

Not so with spring. Spring finds flowers popping up where barren icy earth once lay. Spring finds new life bursting forth from its hibernation, scratching its belly and stretching in the wonder of it all. Spring finds surprise everywhere we look—even within our-selves.

"It is always springtime in a heart filled with love."

—Saint John Vianney

We all know, on a rational level, that spring follows winter. We can experience each year the gloomy darkness of days giving way to the lengthening of light, the cold air giving way to warmth, the barren ground giving way to delicious life.

But the transition from the winter of our discontent to the spring of hope and promise can be much more difficult to make. How can it be, we wonder, that a heart so painfully hard and cold due to loss, can ever be warm again? The answer is through love, and only through love. Because only by being mindful of the love that was, the love that is, and the love that will be can hearts broken be made whole, and wondrous life burst forth from what once was cold and dark.

22

"When Jesus heard of the death of John the Baptizer, he withdrew by boat from there to a deserted place by himself."

—Matthew 14:13-21

His cousin was dead. Their relationship began with the Baptizer dancing in the womb of his mother at the presence of his cousin, also in the womb. Their relationship was sealed in the Jordan, when the two of them swirled into the waters. And their relationship was ended with a mother's vengeful spite, and a girl's frenzied dance. And, to make sense of it all, to express that grief that tore at His heart, Jesus had to be alone.

But after this, the gospel tells us, He went on to five thousand people. Perhaps He realized that, although the amazing dance begun so long ago had ended, there were still people around who needed to be fed. Perhaps He knew that in remembering the dead, He could not neglect the needs of the living.

"But Mary kept all these things, pondering them in her heart."

—Luke 2:19

My Gramps was a real storyteller, and I used to sit in fascination while he recounted stories of his colorful life over a cup of coffee and a game of solitaire. Gramps' stories were real, and I learned a great deal about life and who I am while drinking in the wonder of his words, of his memories.

Memories, it's true, can be painful. But it is important that, in trying to heal our grief, we don't allow ourselves to keep them only in our hearts. Because when we remember someone, somehow they are still with us. And if we can recognize this presence, then death will never have the final word, for the story will continue in us.

24

"But the angel said to him, 'Do not be afraid, Zechariah, for your prayer is heard, and your wife Elizabeth will bear you a son, and you shall call his name John.'"

—Luke 1:13

How amazing that it happened, how seemingly impossible. Zechariah and Elizabeth, now advancing in years, had most likely resigned themselves to the fact that they would have no children. In a place and time where it was felt that if you couldn't have children, you must have done something wrong, they had quietly endured the talk, the pity. And with each passing year the hope that had burned so brightly at the beginning of their life together grew more and more dim. And then it happened. Elizabeth, thought to be sterile, was pregnant, and that light of hope that had been all but extinguished now grew and blazed inside of her. How amazing that it happened, how seemingly impossible. But you see, nothing is impossible with God.

"And Mary said to the angel, 'How shall this be, since I have no husband?'"
—Luke 1:34

How amazing that it happened, how seemingly impossible. Mary, a young girl, is visited by an angel of God, with an astounding message: God wanted to be born into the world and into frail humanity. And to help bring this about, he chose a young girl, and asked her to agree to all of this wonder, this confusion. And this young girl said yes to the will of God, and the womb of a virgin now nurtured a child. How amazing that it happened. How seemingly impossible. But you see, nothing is impossible with God.

26

"For with God, nothing will be impossible."

—Luke 1:37

Perhaps in recounting the stories of Mary and Elizabeth every year they have lost their power to truly captivate, to make us aware of the possibilities that exist in the seemingly impossible. This is sad, for we frequently need to be reminded of these possibilities, need to see the seemingly impossible tasks of healing and forgiveness as possibilities. Because the same God who allowed a barren old woman to conceive; the same God who could bring forth a baby from the womb of a virgin; this God can bring to birth in us possibilities that are seemingly impossible, if we trust and believe like Elizabeth, like Mary. How amazing the things we could achieve, how seemingly impossible the tasks we can undertake. Because nothing is impossible with God.

"And silence, like a poultice, comes / To heal the blows of sound."

—Oliver Wendell Holmes

One of the things about monastic life about which people are the most curious is our emphasis on silence. We eat breakfast in silence. We don't speak in the hallways. We eat dinner without speaking, while listening to a book being read. We don't talk before church in the morning or after 10:00 p.m. at night. The emphasis on silence for monks is usually linked to interior stillness so as better to hear the voice of God.

But silence—not just for monks, but for anyone—can also help us put things in perspective. When the world is assaulting us with noise, it is in true silence that we can begin to hear what is really important, what is really touching us at that moment, what we need to do. And what is this perspective, this insight, if not the voice of God?

*"Si monumentum requiris circumspice
[If you would see the man's monument,
look around.]"*

—Inscription in Saint Paul's Cathedral, London
written by the son of architect Sir Christopher
Wren

To most tourists in London it is a destination, the beautiful Saint Paul's Cathedral, site of the wedding of Charles and Diana all those years ago. It is an amazing building, grand symmetry singing of the perfection of God; high adorned dome singing of humankind's need to praise God. It is a breathtaking monument to the reality of all things being possible in God.

So too, it is a monument to Sir Christopher Wren, and, through him, to us all. For not only does it speak of the wonders of God's amazing love, it also speaks of the amazing things we can achieve when we allow ourselves to be enveloped in that love.

"To be able to enjoy one's past life is to live twice."

—Martial

During my ordination to the priesthood, as I was lying prostrate on the floor of the cathedral, I was overcome with sadness. Here I was, on the most important day of my life, and two of the most significant people in my life—my mother and my grandmother—were not there to celebrate with me. In the midst of this painful realization, a barrage of images from my past exploded within my mind: My mother opening her gifts at Christmastime, my grandmother enfolding me in the warmth of her fleshy arms, meals where I was happily placed between both of them at the table. And as I heard the cantor recounting the names of great saints who have been witnesses to the faith throughout the ages, I realized that my memory of these two women was a testimony to their witness of the salvific power of love.

"If life had a second edition, how I would correct the proofs."

—John Clare

If only I had more often said I love you, or thank you, or I appreciate who you are, or I like who I am when I am with you, or you are so important to me. If only I hadn't said some of the hateful things I did. If only I had done more for you, with you. If only I hadn't done the things that I did that were hurtful.

Life can be filled with regret, and how nice it would be if we could have that second edition, correct the proofs. But the harsh reality is that we cannot, that things said and done, things left unsaid and undone, are in the past, and there is absolutely nothing we can do to change them.

Except, of course, accept their lessons, thus changing the present.

"Heaven is under our feet as well as over our heads."

—Henry David Thoreau

Each year during Lent, one of my resolutions is to take a walk to our cemetery each day. The cemetery is located in a quiet area surrounded by pine trees with a small lake nearby, and the calmness of it all—the water, the trees, the cool spring air—helps me put things in perspective. I realize that my daily struggles, seemingly so pressing at the time, don't seem so terrible there.

It is also clear to me that there, in the dark indifference of the earth, rests the bodies of those who had their own struggles and joys in this same place. They, too, perhaps walked to this very place, to help them make sense of it all, to help calm them. And as my feet trod the grass-covered ground that separates me from them, it dawns on me how really very little at all separates us.

APRIL

"Flowers are lovely; love is flower-like; friendship a sheltering tree."
—Samuel Taylor Coleridge

Not too long ago I was at a retreat center in Victoria, Texas, or, more accurately, in the middle of nowhere near Victoria, Texas. There was on the grounds the largest oak tree I had ever seen. The caretaker of the center swore that it had been around since the time of Christ, but other estimates put it at maybe 800 years old. Regardless of its true age, it was absolutely beautiful, its gnarled trunk and expansive leafiness a testimony to steadfastness, permanence.

Coleridge was right in likening friendship to such a tree. There might be people in the world more beautiful, more colorful, more flower-like than our friends, to be sure. But no one can shelter us the way our friends can and do.

2

"God said, 'Come no nearer! Remove the sandals from your feet, for the place where you stand is holy ground.'"

—Exodus 3:5

How would we react, standing face to face with God, hearing His voice echo throughout the air like thunder from on high, quaking with fear at the mere thought of being so near the Creator? How would we feel to be so intensely close to the Father of all the living?

We could answer these questions by asking more questions: How do we react when God visits us daily in the graced moments of our lives? How closely do we listen to His voice when we hear it in those around us, in the still sorrow of our own hearts? How do we feel when we experience the God of all the living visiting us, even in the guise of the sick and dying?

Moses recognized who it was that was speaking to him. Do we?

"They say everything in the world is good for something."

—John Dryden

I wouldn't describe myself as a pack-rat, but on the other hand I do hate to throw anything away. Rummaging through the office or my room, mindful of needing to get rid of things, I still nevertheless hesitate to get rid of anything, because, even though not a full-fledged pack-rat myself, I am nonetheless haunted by the Eternal Question of the Pack-Rat: What if I need this later?

There is something to be said for keeping our eyes (and ears and hearts) open for those things (and people) that will be able to help us later, indeed, may even be helping us right now.

4

"Is it not to you alone, O Lord, to whom we look?"

—Jeremiah 14:22

Sometimes it is best just not to ask too many questions. Take the people of the prophet Jeremiah's day: Did they really want the Lord to answer the question of where they looked to? The answer was that they were looking everywhere but to the Lord. They looked to idols, as if mere images of gold could fill the emptiness that was within them. They looked to sinful deeds, as if in these actions they would find what they were searching for. They shouldn't have asked, if they didn't want to hear the answers.

What about us? Is it to the Lord alone that we look? Do we have the courage to ask this same question?

"But when [Peter] perceived how strong the wind was, becoming frightened, he began to sink and cried out, 'Lord, save me!'"

—Matthew 14:29

There had to have been a million voices running through his head: "You can't walk on water." Undeterred, Peter did just that, and sank only when he lost sight of his goal, when he took too much stock in the voices that besieged him.

Similar voices might speak to us as well, the loudest of which are the voices of our own souls: "You can't get over this. It's too much." Undeterred, we need to confidently move forward. And when we feel that we might be sinking in a flood of grief, we must remember to keep our eyes firmly planted on our goal.

"*God's finger touched him, and he slept.*"

—Alfred, Lord Tennyson

Anyone who knows me well, knows that I am not to be disturbed on Sunday afternoons, when I retire for a full-force, pajamas-on, under-the-covers nap. The cares, the concerns of life don't seem to matter for a couple of hours, and my spirit and soul can escape and be refreshed. Everything waits for me when I awake, but for a while I know great peace.

Poets and writers have often linked death to sleeping, and that used to disturb me, because it brought with it images of unsuccessfully trying to awaken someone, which is a sad notion. But if I can make myself reflect on the sheer peace of a nap, and imagine awakening, not to the struggles of life, but to a continuation of the peace of the nap, then maybe linking death with sleep isn't so bad.

"Jesus told [Thomas]: 'I am the way, the truth and the life.'"

—John 14:6

L ord, I feel lost. At times I think I know where I am going, feel I am on the right path, and at other times I'm not so sure. How can I know where it is I am supposed to be? "I am the way."

Lord, I feel confused. Things that I have long taken for granted don't seem so certain anymore. With so many different messages assailing my ears, how can I be certain which message is the true one? "I am the truth."

Lord, I feel beaten. Sadness and loss have so clouded my vision that I can no longer seem to see eternity, but am mired instead with viewing only the harsh realities that are in front of me. With so much death, how can I be certain that everything just doesn't end? "I am the life."

So many questions. One answer: I Am.

"Suddenly the curtain of the sanctuary was torn in two from top to bottom. The earth quaked, boulders split, tombs opened."

—Matthew 26:51-52

It is the story of one man, and yet the story of all humanity. It is a story that happened in an isolated part of the world, and yet a story that the universe could not contain. It is a story, the tragedy of which made the angels of God weep, and yet caused them to sing songs of exultation heard around the world throughout the ages. It is a story of treacherous complexity, and yet a story of love, wondrously simple. It is the story of Jesus Christ, and yet it is our story: the story of our desires, our failings, our hopes, our sadness, our longings, our lives. It is only through this story that the stories of our lives have any meaning. It is this story that makes us who we are. And so we need to carry it all—our pain, struggle, grief, hope— and go up to Jerusalem with the Lord, to let our story become one with his story.

"When Jesus took the wine, he said, 'Now it is finished.' Then he bowed his head, and delivered over his spirit."

—John 19:30

Good Friday can be a somewhat unnerving day. So many of the images of the Savior with which we surround ourselves stand quiet today. Christ the King, Christ the Victor, Christ the Conqueror over evil—these are images that comfort us, that can make us feel as if things are in control in a world that we know is far from being in control. What images of the Savior do we regard on this day? That of the suffering servant of Isaiah. We are asked this day to let go of some of our more comforting images of Jesus, and immerse ourselves in the paradox of the Savior of the world submitting to the agony and shame of a common criminal's death, the paradox of the Cross. In one sense, how tragic, how pitiful that cross. But in another sense, the sense of faith, how splendid is that cross. It brings light, not darkness; Paradise, not its loss; life, not death.

"*On the first day of the week, at dawn, the women came to the tomb bringing the spices they had prepared.*"
—Luke 24:1

There are times, it seems, in the midst of a world that can confuse and hurt us, when sorrow can be almost soothing. Many things in this world might change, but the real human grief that can affect us all is often constant, for a while anyway. Surely this is one of the things that motivated Mary Magdalene and the other women to go to that tomb the first morning of the week. It had been a confusing, painful three days, full of turmoil and pain, and now they were going to go to the place where they had laid him, to sit with their sorrow, to be soothed by their tears. Because they knew, that even if the last three years of following this man had been a series of often times confusing ups and downs, here, in the cool mist of the morning and in the cool mist of their grief, there was no confusion. There was the ages-old consolation of those who mourn.

"They found the stone rolled back from the tomb; but when they entered the tomb, they did not find the body of the Lord Jesus."

—Luke 24:2-3

But the women soon found out that now, in the quiet of death, there still was confusion, turmoil. Because the tomb was not as it had been left. The huge stone was rolled away. And so they worriedly ran off to the rest of the disciples, to see if they could put their confusing world back in order somehow, to bring back the calm. And they, too, were shocked and confused. But John, we read elsewhere, saw and believed. And at that moment he realized: nothing would ever be calm, nothing would ever be ordinary again. Life, as he knew it, had changed. Because in a world where darkness was all too prevalent, light triumphed. In a world where hatred and division were the order of the day, peace was victorious. And in a world where all die, death was rendered impotent.

12

*"Protect us by thy might, Great God
our King!"*

—Samuel Francis Smith

One night while in Texas I was walking along a path back to the cabin
in which I was staying when I heard
some clicking noise right behind me. I
turned around, and at my feet, apparently as startled as I, was an armadillo. I had
never seen one before, and was fascinated by this curious little animal, amazed
at how extensive its armor seemed to be.

It helps, especially during times
when we feel the most vulnerable, to
reflect just how like an armadillo we
really are. Instead of hard shells on the
outside of our skin, we need to content
ourselves with the fact that we have been
provided with the armor of friendship,
love, memories, joy—all gifts from a
God who longs to protect us, curious little animals that we are.

"Wisely, and slow. They stumble that run fast."

—William Shakespeare

The invention of the microwave has affected the way we live. Gone are the days when making a TV dinner used to take 45 minutes; now it can be dispatched in a mere ten minutes—Salisbury steak steaming, potatoes a bit crusted, apple cobbler downright molten. Often now we expect all things to be dispatched this quickly, giving into the microwave mentality of the harried, slapdash world in which we live.

God's ways are different, of course. If society holds up the image of a microwave as the norm, God's image is rather of a slow-cooking stew, stirred by a loving cook who wants to make sure that all the ingredients—sweet and bitter—take enough time to really complete the taste. We might not like some of the ingredients, but if we trust the cook we know in the end we'll be filled indeed.

*"The holiest of all holidays are those /
Kept by ourselves in silence and apart;
The secret anniversaries of the heart."*
—Henry Wadsworth Longfellow

My grandmother died on February 14. Each year when the whole country remembers the romantic love that is a staple of Valentine's Day, I remember a different kind of love. I remember her cooking supper as I sat with my Gramps. I remember being enveloped in her soft embrace, while she exclaimed, "You're my baby!" I remember her getting so tickled at something that her laughter would bring about tears and then, apparently on a dime, she would start crying for real, remembering something that saddened her. I remember it all, and I celebrate both the life and the loss. Some would say dwelling year after year on thoughts that ultimately make me sad is tapping into some sort of warped masochism. They can think that. I know I am tapping into holiness.

"For me you have changed my mourning into dancing, you removed my sackcloth and girded me with joy."
—Psalm 29

It seems a little far-fetched to me. The slow shuffling of feet weighted down by sadness, replaced by the twirling dance of new life, of hope? The melancholy apparel of sorrowing, replaced by the bright garments of joy? Can it really be like this? It seems awfully difficult to believe that it can.

But believe we are asked to do. And as a guide to our belief, we have the example of one whose sad dragging of feet through the streets of Jerusalem was replaced by the ecstatic dance of the Resurrection. We have the example of the one whose dark, blood-stained garments were replaced by the brightness of glory.

Far-fetched? Perhaps. Real? Most definitely, if we allow ourselves to join in His dance.

"O the idea was childish, but divinely beautiful."

—Johann Christoph Friedrich von Schiller

Once when taking my dog on a walk on a summer's day, I encountered some children climbing trees a few blocks from my house. I smiled at how much fun they were having, remembering how delightful it was for me to do the same thing when I was their age: above it all, surrounded by the leafy familiarity of my favorite tree, not a care in the world.

Upon returning home I noticed, two yards over, a tree that would have been the perfect climbing tree, if I were still a child, still involved in that sort of endeavor. And before I knew it, I was involved in that sort of endeavor. People might have thought I was crazy, but I didn't care. There *is* something divinely beautiful about the childish, and I think we need to tap into that every now and then.

"Not Truth, but Faith it is / That keeps the world alive."

—Edna St. Vincent Millay

We have faith that the sun will rise tomorrow. We have faith that the just are eventually rewarded and the bad get theirs in the end. We have faith that God is somehow mysteriously active in the world. We have faith that the world can still be a good place. We have faith that next year—maybe, just maybe—the Cubs could win a pennant. We have faith that our friends will be there for us. If we truly sit down and reflect on what faith we put in ourselves, in others, in our world we'll usually find that we have more faith than we might see at first glance. If we can have so much faith at so many times in our lives, we should know we can have faith in even the more difficult times of our lives. And truly this faith can keep us—and our world—alive.

18 *"The gift you have received, give as gift."*

—Matthew 10: 8

I got much of my love of books from my mother. I got much of my love of storytelling from my grandfather. I got much of my love of receiving mushy affection from my grandmother. And so it is, that every time I write something, or share something I'm reading with a friend; every time I tell a story, trying to achieve that twinkle in my brown eyes that was clearly present in Gramps' blue eyes; every time I am unafraid to let down my guard and show unbridled affection for someone I love; a part of my mother, my grandfather and my grandmother lives on in me. And at those moments they don't seem so far away.

"Creativity is more important than knowledge."

—Albert Einstein

When I was in kindergarten I made a necklace for my mother out of paper clips covered in orange and brown patterned contact paper. I realize now, of course, that it was hideous, but at the time I thought it quite beautiful and was inordinately proud of it. My sense of pride absolutely exploded within me when, getting ready for a party one evening, she chose the necklace as the perfect compliment for her evening wear.

We spend a great deal of time trying to *know* what it is we need to know: how to do our work, how to deal with others, how to get beyond things in life that are weighing us down. But somewhere, in the midst of all of our knowledge, we also must realize that the sheer wonder of creating something—a painting, a poem, anything—can bring much more beauty (and, I think, perspective) into our lives than a thousand textbooks can.

"He said not, 'Thou shall not be tempested, thou shall not be travailed, thou shall not be diseased;' but he said, 'Thou shall not be overcome.'"

—Julian of Norwich

"I never promised you a rose garden," the popular song goes, and most of us can agree. Jesus makes it pretty clear what he promises those who will follow Him: hardship, trial, persecution. We feel sometimes that what we get is, not the rose, but the thorn. And so we struggle, trying to make sense of it all, trying to keep our head above ground, as we seek to grow in spite of some severe pruning.

Of course, we need never lose sight of another of the Lord's promises: I will be with you until the end of time. Life, for all its thorns and brambles, cannot completely bury us, for He is with us. And even after the day when life finally does bury us, we know that He is still with us, as the thorns of this life give way to the most beautiful rose of eternity.

"*What in me is dark / Illumine, what is low raise and support.*"

—John Milton

It's a simple prayer, and one that can easily find voice on the lips of so many of us. There are those places within us, shaded by fear, darkened by grief, tinted by confusion, that long to be enlightened, but we do not always know how to allow the light to pierce the darkness. There are those times in our lives when we feel low, burdened with sorrow, nearly crushed with grief, and we long to be raised above it all.

And so we pray to be enlightened, to be lifted up. And it can seem at times that God stands monstrously silent at these times, but it is a silence that perhaps asks us to look, not listen: to look at a man burdened with a cross, lifted up, who has become the very light of the world. It won't always make us feel better, this answer, but it is the only answer we've got.

"Frost and chill bless the Lord, praise and exalt him above all forever."

—Daniel 3: 69

The spring weather had been pleasant, mild and sunny. Not only the early-risers like the daffodils decided to emerge from the winter's sleep, but the more cautious tulips had made their appearance on the scene as well. All around were the enchanting colors of the season—the greens just a little more green; the yellows and reds just a little more so.

And then, it happened: the frost. A killing frost that came in the midst of the loveliness to announce that winter was not so far removed. And many of us resented it, this frost, resented its ugly arrival on a scene that had been all too beautiful. Begrudgingly, however, we had to admit: this frost somehow came from God as well as the beauty, and was so connected to the beauty that there couldn't quite be a real recognition of one without the other.

> "*The* Israelites lamented, 'Would that we had meat for food! ... But now we are famished; we see nothing before us but this manna.'"
>
> —Numbers 11:4-6

First they were in slavery in Egypt and the Lord led them out, going so far as to part the sea to get them to safety. Then they were hungry, and the Lord rained down manna from heaven for them so that all they had to do was pick it up in the morning and they would have food. Then, even the manna wasn't enough; they wanted meat. It all smacks just a bit of ingratitude. But then they had been through a great deal and they still weren't where they ultimately wanted to be, and gratitude isn't always easy when you're in a place you don't want be.

This same patience should be extended to us as well, when we find that we are weary from the journey and have yet to reach our destination. Perhaps a little grumbling is fine, as long as we remember that we, like this original group of grumblers, will too reach our destination.

"But I have promises to keep, / And miles to go before I sleep, And miles to go before I sleep."

—Robert Frost

"How can I go on?" she asked me, standing at the open casket of her husband of 37 years. I wanted to answer, but wasn't sure the time was right to tell her. You'll go on, I wanted to say, because the human spirit has an amazing resiliency. You'll go on, I wanted to say, because you're stubborn. You'll go on, I wanted to say, because the alternative just won't do. You'll go on, I wanted to say, because even if life seems horrid and frightening and unfair and wretched right now, you know that, in addition to all those things, it can be not-half-bad as well. I wanted to say it all, but instead I just said, "I don't know, I don't know," and held her hand. She seemed to think it a good enough answer at the time.

"Remember, man, that you are dust, and unto dust you shall return."

—Formula for the distribution of ashes, Ash Wednesday

On Ash Wednesday as Christians come forward in church to receive the sign of ashes on their foreheads, thus beginning the penitential season of Lent, most thoughts are turned to sorrow for sin, and firm amends to try and live better lives. Another formula—"turn away from sin and be faithful to the gospel"—ties in with this, and, perhaps because these particular words seem so fitting, this is the option that seems most often used.

I, personally, like the dust imagery better. Because in recognizing that we, too, shall some day turn to dust, we are keeping the precious, limited nature of life before our eyes—always a good thing. But also, too, foreheads smudged, we are mindful of those who have already gone before us, and just how like them, and connected to them, we all are.

"Everywhere, we learn only from those whom we love."

—Goethe

I began kindergarten at age 5 and, basically, went to school full time for the next 22 years. I'm one of those people who actually likes schooling, which is obviously a good thing. There is so much to be learned, so much information to gather, that I suspect I will in some aspects be a student my whole life.

Life's most important lessons, however, can rarely be learned from books. How nice it would be if, when mourning, when questioning why, when giving in to anger, we could turn to a book that would help us put things in perspective, help us make sense of it all, help us know unequivocally why things in our life went the way they did. More often than not, with the possible exception of the Bible, books can't help us a whole lot.

But people clearly can.

"All work and no play makes Jack a dull boy."

—James Howell

This is one of those lines that has been around for a while, but I was never sure how long. Surely it is a modern quote, as only we post-industrial moderns are obsessed with work in such a way as it can rule our life, right? Wrong. The words were written in 1659, showing that our desire to keep busy—often to a fault—is something that apparently we have been about the business of for some time.

We work for so many reasons: to get ahead; to be able to afford things for our family and children; to assure ourselves security down the road; to somehow express who we are.

But if we work to forget or escape, then perhaps we should reflect on what it is we want to forget, escape, and sharpen our ability to cope in other ways—ways like God, family, and friendship.

"*Bliss in possession will not last; /
Remembered joys are never past.*"
—James Montgomery

One of my favorite pictures from our family album shows my parents and my father's cousin and her husband mugging for the camera with goofy, hysterical faces. My mother's presence in a robe, looking frail, is a testimony to the fact that it was obviously taken at a time when happiness was probably in short supply. So much in the picture is no longer around; we've lived in several different houses since then; we have new furniture, new drapes, new lamps; my father's cousin is no longer married to the man in the picture; my mother is no longer alive. But for all the transitory things that are there in that faded Polaroid, the sheer joy of the moment will never die.

"Rock of Ages, cleft for me,
Let me hide myself in thee."
—Augustus Montague Toplady

When I was young and would have bad dreams I would cover my head completely under the covers, thinking that, ordinarily, the monsters of childhood couldn't hurt me if they couldn't see me. On occasion, though, that wouldn't work, and I would rush out of bed into my parents' room. If the occasional monster could somehow penetrate my covers, it most certainly couldn't penetrate those of my parents and I would rest peacefully there until I would awake the next day, mysteriously back in my own bed.

The monsters of the adult world—regret, fear, loss, anxiety—aren't so easily vanquished, it seems at first glance. But if we realize that we still can hide ourselves in the loving familiarity of our God, then we may find the monsters don't have the final say, and peaceful rest can be ours.

30

"Now is the acceptable time! Now is the day of salvation!"

—2 Corinthians 6:2

All too often, to be able to understand—or at least take—suffering a little better, we look to the future: I know that this is going to make me stronger someday, I just have to hold out until then. In all of this, we keep our eyes and hearts firmly planted on the goal of the future, when the pain will be gone and in its place strength will be ours.

It is important for us to realize that although it might be natural to wish for a day when the pain will be gone, we must never lose sight that right now, in this moment we wish were over, God's grace is powerfully present. To paraphrase that other Lewis writer, C.S., the pain we experience now and the beauty of that future moment are connected; the beauty then is a part of the pain now, and vice versa. And seeing this, not wishing it away, is the real grace of suffering.

MAY

"Your attitude must be Christ's."
—Philippians 2:5

We can be stubborn, all of us. We can hold to our own thoughts and our way of doing things with dogged tenacity, as if we have all the answers, as if no one else knows quite as much as we do. We can firmly plant our feet where we are, refusing to move forward, refusing to heed the voices of those who may call us forward. We can hold our own self-will as the model for how we—and a great part of the world—should react. We can do all of this, and at one time or another, we probably have.

Or, we can have Christ's attitude, who realized that His will had to be also the will of the Father; who knew that to really be filled He had to empty Himself; who knew that to really live He had to die; who knew that to really be exalted He had to be brought low.

Our attitude seems so much easier, but is ultimately less successful.

"If you live according to my teaching, you are truly my disciples; then you will know the truth, and the truth will set you free."

—John 8:31-32

"Truth hurts!" I remember hearing kids yell on the playground, to punctuate a nasty comment that had preceded it. And truly there can be something remotely painful about the truth which can slap us in the face with reality, even when we would rather not know the real story; which can lay bare all white lies, making them appear not-so-white after all. Yes, truth can indeed hurt.

That's why Jesus' offer of the truth, with the added promise that we will somehow be set free by it, can be a bit jarring for those of us who have said, from time to time, "What they don't know won't hurt them." Indeed, Jesus seems to be saying, what we don't know can indeed hurt us, and then, even after we know, the truth can continue to hurt us. Of course, as is the case with Jesus, His pain brings healing and promise.

*"It is a wonderful seasoning of all
enjoyments to think of those we love."*
—Molière

3

M
A
Y

I was one of those children who actually liked going to school. But every now and then, when May would roll around and the robins would taunt me on the sun-drenched lawn outside, the day became a drudgery, something odious to be endured. And so I would look out the window and think of going home, of being with the neighborhood gang and getting into some kind of mischief, of being with my family and sharing a meal and a laugh.

In addition to being an antidote for the malady of a bad day, thinking of the ones we love can also help make a wonderful day all the more wonderful. And so every time I encounter something new and delightful, I think of my family, my friends, and even those people who are no longer with me in this life. And in sharing my happiness with them, I am connected to them.

4

"*For the measure you measure with
will be measured back to you.*"

—Luke 6:36-38

Of all the measurable commodities,
perhaps none is so precious as time.
There are only so many hours in the day,
and there are so many things we feel we
need to do, that making all of it happen
seems daunting, if not downright
impossible. And so it can be that we feel
we just have no time to write a note to
someone we know is suffering, or pay a
visit to someone who really needs support, or even pick up the phone to bol-
ster the drooping spirits of another.

If we don't make time for these people, however, we might just find that
others won't make time for us when we
suffer, when we need support, when our
spirits droop. Time, as precious as it is,
demands to be shared with others, not
hoarded.

"'Tut, tut, child,' said the Duchess. 'Everything's got a moral if only you can find it.'"

—Lewis Carroll

Some say that everything you need to know you learn in kindergarten. I myself think this is ridiculous, because I, for one, never heard anything about the internet or tax breaks—for instance—in kindergarten. I would be much more comfortable to modify the statement to: Everything you need to know you learn in life. And how true this is. Through the death of my mother I learned how precious life is. Through my own illness I learned to appreciate health. Through confusion and doubt I have learned to believe. I guess it would be nice if all of our lessons could be like in kindergarten—complete with snack time, a nap, and story time. But it is ultimately more rewarding, I think, to find the moral in life by living out the story, not just hearing about it.

5

M

A

Y

"*Batter my heart, three-person'd God; for you / As yet but knock, breathe, shine, and seek to mend.*"

—John Donne

It may not always be pleasant, the way that God does indeed knock on our hearts, battering us with His persistent Spirit until we acquiesce and let Him in. God's knocking can take so many different forms, even the sorrow of loss. For in our longing to be with someone, we are giving voice to that ultimate longing wherein we long to be united with God. It's hard to see this, though, when our hearts are battered. But infinitely easier when they are mended, which can only happen when we acknowledge the One at the door.

"He who created you without you will justify you without you."

—Augustine of Hippo

I'm angry with You, God, I said, and I want nothing to do with You. Oh, but I am everything to do with you, said God. I hurt, God, I said, and You seem to be the cause. Oh, but in your pain is my love, said God. I am confused, God, and You seem nothing but a mystery with no chance of solving. Oh, but in the mystery is the answer to everything, said God. I miss them, O God, and You apparently took them from me. Oh, but in the emptiness of your heart you can still have them, said God.

I can't seem to get away from You, God, I said. Oh, but you're right, said God. And love was the language of it all.

"Strike the rock, and the water will flow from it for the people to drink."

—Exodus 17:6

One of my favorite stories is *The Selfish Giant* by Oscar Wilde, wherein a nasty, selfish giant's stony heart is touched by the love of a very special child, and his life here (and in the hereafter) is changed forever. The moral of the story is that Christ can make love spring forth from even the hardest of hearts.

We need to believe that. We need to believe that even if our hearts seem rock-hard, the awareness of Christ can change our hearts, bringing solace where there was sorrow, forgiveness where there was resentment, peace where there was turmoil. Hearts of stone thus pierced, we can then go on to help quench the thirst of others with the beautiful, refreshing grace that had been flooded over us.

"Reading is to the mind what exercise is to the body."

—Joseph Addison

The first book I remember reading was *The Wind in the Willows* by Kenneth Grahame. It is a wonderful book, filled with joy and treachery and love and envy and, in the end, peace. I remember slowly making my way through the book with my mother, enthralled by this discovery that these letters on a page could combine and reach right into my soul, could give voice to the joy and treachery and love and envy and peace that I experienced in my own life.

Good writers tell stories in ways that, even though the story is uniquely theirs, we can nevertheless see ourselves in as well. And so what a worthwhile exercise it is to open a book in our constant attempt to understand the stories of our lives.

10

"The people struck their tents to cross the Jordan, with the priests carrying the ark of the covenant ahead of them."
—Joshua 3:14

It had been a long journey, beginning with slavery in Egypt and deliverance from Pharaoh's bonds, to the vast expansiveness of the wilderness. It had been filled with confusion and doubt, with wondering what exactly their God had gotten them into. And yet, they heard over and over for a generation that He would deliver them, and so they marched on, and came to this point, where they crossed the Jordan and finally entered into that land which had been promised them so long ago.

Even in the midst of some backsliding, they stuck with their God, and He delivered them. He will do the same for us.

"*Then they recounted what had happened on the road and how they had come to recognize him in the breaking of the bread.*"

—Luke 24:35

On a lonesome, dusty road, some saddened men encounter a stranger. They tell Him the story of their sadness, how they had put their hope in this Jesus and He had been executed like a common criminal. And now, when they just wanted to deal with it all, friends were saying that His tomb was empty, causing all kinds of confusion. The stranger talks to them, to try to help their confusion, to help them put their world back in order. And then, in the midst of these ordinary men with ordinary woes, the stranger breaks ordinary bread in their midst and suddenly they realize that what appears ordinary is not ordinary at all, but Jesus Himself breaking through with His extraordinary presence.

It is important to pay attention to the ordinary, because one never knows what might come of it.

"*He told me everything I ever did.*"

—John 4:39

It can be a bit unnerving, thinking of an all-knowing, all-present, all-seeing God. Those of us who were raised on the American ideals of freedom and individuality just might balk at the image of a God who is always watching us, like Orwell's Big Brother. It can seem a bit invasive.

Or comforting. Because what a solace it can be to think that God knows all of our struggles, our sufferings, our confusion, our fear. What relief to know that, even if we battle something over and over again, God is there for every battle, and knows what a toll other such battles have taken on us. If we survived them then, it was due in large part to this all-knowing, all-present, all-seeing God, passionately in love with us, intimately involved. And knowing this can help us survive the same things now.

"Fading, fading; strength beyond hope and despair ..."

—T. S. Eliot

Not long after his father died, my friend James was in the grocery store, in that strange place where the extraordinary peculiarity of the loss of a loved one exists side by side with the routine of everyday life. His father's unexpected death had been just one more in a series of crushing blows, and his very faith was admittedly shaken to its core. Maybe years of prayer and trying to live the Christian life just weren't worth it, he found himself thinking.

"Paper or plastic?" the check-out girl asked, the mundane question jolting him temporarily out of his deep despair. He looked up to answer, and saw that her name tag said, "Hope." And he did.

14

"God is love."

—1 John 4:8

One time in a college morality class, the professor turned the discussion to love. We had, at this point, studied all kinds of philosophical definitions of love. We spent what seemed like weeks on the writings of Augustine. And so, wanting, I suppose, a synthesis of what we had learned to that point, he asked the class, "What is love?" Then he called on James.

James opened his mouth and sputtered and stuttered so much that intelligible speech could not be heard—it almost sounded like a groan. The professor moved on to someone else, who answered the question more to his liking.

I can't help but think, however, that James' answer probably hit closer to the mark. If God is love, then love is eternal, loving, all-knowing, and—not just a little bit—confusing.

"Where'er we tread 'tis haunted, holy ground."

—George Noel Gordon, Lord Byron

After the death of Joseph Cardinal Bernardin, my friends David and Stephanie and I decided to drive three and a half hours to pay our respects to this man who had meant so much to us in different ways. And so began our journey to Chicago, a journey that we had made countless times before for Cubs games, Bulls games, weekend get-aways, and social engagements.

This time, the road was different, however. Boring Interstate 57 suddenly seemed a beautiful road, made significant by our pilgrimage.

We sometimes tend to limit holiness to churches, or grand, lush scenes. But any path upon which we walk—any path which leads us to significant moments of grace and insight—has the ability to be an avenue of holiness, if we pay attention to the journey.

"Who would have thought my shrivel'd heart / Could have recovered greenness?"

—George Herbert

My mother died in the summer, at a time when a young boy's thoughts should be turned to games of baseball and hide-and-seek. A few days after the funeral, life once again returned to some semblance of routine: Dad worked, we went to church, but I couldn't bring myself to go out and play, even though the very nature of summer seemed to demand it. No, I would never play again, I was determined. It might as well have been winter, my young heart was so cold.

But slowly the rays of the sun enticed me through the windows and I ventured outside. And, breathing in the exciting possibilities of a summer's day, I found my way to my neighbor's house, to see if maybe something was going on. My life would never be the same, I knew, but it could be good again, I decided. And so I ran to get my bicycle.

"I will look to the Lord, I will put my trust in God my savior; my God will hear me!"

—Micah 7:7

It can seem as if God doesn't always care. It can seem as if we have to bear our sorrow alone. It can seem as if God doesn't listen to our prayers. And when it seems this way, we need to pray for the grace to realize that the sun rising each morning to bathe us in light is a sign that God cares; a smile brushing ever-so-briefly across our lips is a sign that God sends joy into our lives; the feeling, however fleeting, that the people we love are somehow encouraged and protected by that love is a sign that our prayers are indeed heard.

Life goes much smoother and seems to make more sense if we look to the Lord—and His signs—first, before anything else.

"*The earth, and every common sight, /
To me did seem / Appareled in celestial
light.*"

—William Wordsworth

When I was in junior high school, I
spent a lot of time on the phone.
Perhaps my favorite conversations, however, were with my friend Stephanie,
who lived across the street. If I used the
phone at my father's desk upstairs, and
she used the phone in her living room,
we could sit in our respective windows
and look at each other while we talked.
That we could have easily hung up, gone
out our front doors, and spoken in person didn't seem to be as fun; perhaps
what made it more interesting is that we
were able to see one another using a
manner of communication that ordinarily involved only talking and listening.

So often in prayer we try to commu-
nicate with a God we cannot see.
Perhaps if we also reflect on the God we
can see—the face of a cherished friend, a
painted sky at sunset—it might all be
more interesting.

"The community of believers were of one mind and one heart."

—Acts of the Apostles 4:32

How was it that a frightened, mostly uneducated group of people in a remote part of the world two thousand years ago could pass on a message that has not only survived all this time, but has gone on to change the world and the scope of human history as we know it? How was it that the Early Church survived in the face of horrific setbacks, oppression, and persecution? Through the Spirit, of course, but specifically through the Spirit binding them together in love, so that they realized they were in it all together.

When we find ourselves saying, "I can do this on my own," we obviously haven't learned the power in being of one mind and heart with others.

"When you have nothing to say, say nothing."

—Charles Caleb Colton

Perhaps one of the biggest misconceptions about prayer is that if we're not doing or saying something, we're not really praying. And so we go about the task of memorizing formulae, of ticking off our prayer lists to God as if we are strolling down the aisle of the grocery store, afraid we'll forget the coffee filters or laundry detergent.

But prayer also occurs when we just don't have anything to say, when the dynamics of life are so confusing that words would only muddy life's waters more. We need to realize that just because we can't bring ourselves to say anything to God in prayer doesn't mean that communication with Him is not there. God's communication with us is like His love for us—eternal—and so silence is not necessarily merely a lack of sound, but a continuation of the conversation that was begun before the ages.

"He called loudly, 'Lazarus, come out!' The dead man came out, bound hand and foot with linen strips, his face wrapped in a cloth. 'Untie him,' Jesus told them, 'and let him go free.'"

—John 11:43-44

It was so long ago, this story of Lazarus with its stifling heat, its oppressive grief, and its miraculous ending. And there is a sense in which we can't relate to the story, we who, unlike Martha and Mary, have had to suffer loss without the outcome of the dead walking back into life. But, if we only view the story from the point of the mourners, we're missing an important point, that being just how like Lazarus we all are. Who among us has not felt dead, shut away in darkness, fettered by the strands of sorrow? And the same Lord comes to us, enters into our stifling heat, our oppressive grief and offers us a miraculous ending: come out.

Lazarus learned what we, too, should know: it is only through encounters with this Jesus that we can be truly free of those things that keep us tied down.

"Throughout, Stephen's face seemed like that of an angel."

—Acts of the Apostles 6:15

He endured the angry words of the crowd, screaming at him to stop preaching of this man named Jesus. He endured imprisonment, put behind bars for believing that this Jesus had risen from the dead. And ultimately he endured death, raising his eyes to heaven and praying for those who would take his life, even as the stones began to assault him. And through all of this, Stephen's face seemed like that of an angel. How was it that he could be so serene, so confident, when fear and loathing surrounded him so violently? It is very difficult for us to understand, we who can fret and worry about so much.

Stephen's strength, of course, came from the fact that he never took his eyes off of the Lord Jesus. How easier our lives could be if we looked in that same direction.

"All experience is an arch, to build upon."

—Henry Brooks Adams

23

M
A
Y

My mother taught me how to read, and what a gift that was, an obvious expression of her love for me. My father taught me to be good to others and to myself, an obvious expression of his love for me. My stepmother taught me to stick with things, even when they didn't go the way I would have liked them to go, an obvious expression of her love for me. And on and on the list goes of people who have taught me because they loved me.

Of course, I cannot deny that I have learned much through the death of my mother, my grandparents, my sister's battle with cancer, as well as my own. And I know that all of these experiences taught me so much, and are an obvious expression of God's love for me. It's just that I don't always understand this kind of love, and so I resist it.

"Nothing in the world is single, / All things by a law divine / In one spirit meet and mingle."

—Percy Bysshe Shelley

One of the cardinal rules of pastoral counseling is to never allow yourself to fall into the trap of saying, "I know how you feel." The way people grieve, the circumstances of loss are as different as people are different. Just because I lost my mother as a young boy, for example, doesn't mean that I presume to know how all young boys who lose their mothers feel.

That being said, however, there is an element of grief that is common to everyone; to suffer is to be human. Every time we feel some sort of suffering or grief in our own lives, it is connected somehow to everyone who suffers, everyone who grieves. And though these nameless, faceless people don't know exactly how we feel, they know that we do feel, because they feel as well.

"Uphold me, O God, according to your promise, and I shall live; and do not confound me in my expectation."

—from the Rite of Monastic Profession
(Psalm 118)

During the presidential election of 1976, President Ford's train was scheduled to make a stop in our small town, population 2500. The day arrived and the preparations were complete: banners made, businesses closed, the high school band present to greet him. The train was seen in the distance, a cry was heard, and as the train drew closer the band struck up their song, while people waved their banners excitedly. The president's train slowed down, but just that—it didn't stop, having, we learned later, gotten too far behind schedule. The crowd stood stunned as the train pulled away. The disappointment was palpable, the dashing of expectations vocalized by the crashing of cymbals.

Life can offer one disappointment after another, but God will always uphold us. He has promised.

*"I have come to the world as its light,
to keep anyone who believes in me from
remaining in the dark."*

—John 12:46

The scene is always the same: a darkened sky, perhaps with streaks of deep red running through it, blustering wind, and three crosses rising up from barren, rocky ground. It is a tragic scene, and the darkness that surrounds it is a link to so much that can frighten us—the darkness of under the bed, the darkness of the closet, the darkness of being lost.

And yet somehow, eventually, the darkness is replaced by a sky streaked by brilliant colors of light, fertile ground, and white garments. And the oppressive fear of the darkness gives way to light, bathing everyone and everything in its path with life, hope, love.

This scene is not just played out in the pages of Scripture and on movie screens. It is played out in the very story of humanity, and its life, hope, and promise, is offered freely to us. We need only believe.

"Jesus said to his disciples, 'Do not let your hearts be troubled.'"

—John 14:1

We all face a legion of worries, often on a daily basis. Basic questions of family struggles, financial concerns, and work pressures often combine with issues of anger, sadness, loss, and confusion. When this occurs, our lives, our thoughts, our hearts can be filled with the constant awareness of the struggle, a constant awareness that life's journey can be arduous, not always easy to manage.

And in the midst of all of this, Jesus tells us not to let our hearts be worried. Is He crazy? Could He really be saying this if He walked in our shoes for a bit? Of course, He *did* walk in our shoes, and, as crazy as it may sound, we *can* have hearts free from trouble if we trust in His presence, if we believe that, as He changed water into wine, He can change us as well.

"I have a song to sing, O! Sing me your song, O!"

—Sir William Schwenck Gilbert

I love to tell stories, talk about things that have happened to me that touched me, things that have shaped me, given me insight into something that just begs for me to share it. I don't tell stories because it's an entertaining thing to do, although it clearly is. I don't tell stories because it's a wonderful way to educate, although it clearly is. No, I tell stories so that somewhere, in my experiences, others may see glimpses of their own experiences, and the memories which can turn into grace in my life may see the same transformation in the lives of those listening to me. And so it is important for us to tell our stories—happy and sad. And not only that, but it is vital that we listen to each others' stories as well. In this exchange, this communication, we get an idea of how connected we all are.

"Save yourself from this generation that has gone astray."
—Acts of the Apostles 2:40

There has been, in the history of monasticism, an "us and them" mentality: monks flee the world and all its wicked ways, while others live in the midst of the wickedness. And when carried to the extreme of viewing the world as inherently bad and the safety of the cloister as more sacred, this mentality is harmful, because it doesn't take into consideration all the wonderful things God can and does do, even in the midst of a crooked world.

This is not to say, however, that all of us, whether we're monks or not, should not resist "the world" in some ways. Because whereas the world can sometimes promote each man for himself, we know the way to go is to care for one another. Whereas the world can tell us that we need to get over it and move on, we know that life is a long journey, a slow process.

"Set your hearts on the greater gifts."
—1 Corinthians 12:31

Not being married myself, it has been a real blessing for me to be able to spend a great deal of time with my friends Marty and Liz. Whether it's looking at their boys' homework or eating pizza and watching movies, their love for each other and their family spills out and envelopes me as well, mirroring God's love, which is what marriage is supposed to be about. What a gift.

I have also been around them, however, in times of struggle, harsh words, and doubt. And, although Marty and Liz might not see it, I realize that these times, too, are somehow a gift. It's just that we often think in our short-sightedness that gifts are only those things that make us feel good. We can sometimes wish to ignore the Cross, which is far from pleasant, but is nevertheless God's love for us spilling out and enveloping us all. What a gift.

"*The ripest peach is highest on the tree.*"

—James Whitcomb Riley

We are all inspired, at one time or another, at stories of little people overcoming enormous obstacles to achieve greatness of some sort. These people are able to achieve what they do because they keep their eyes and hearts firmly planted on the goal in front of them; they will allow nothing that life throws at them to get in the way of their dream. And we are inspired by this because we know just how high the hurdles of life can be that litter our path.

Learning lessons from these people, we begin to realize that keeping our eyes on the goal is the key. How am I going to get through this, over this? we may ask ourselves, looking at each obstacle as insurmountable. But if we can pray for the strength to have our eyes see the end beyond the obstacles, odds are good that we, too, can attain what it is we seek, that ripe peace.

JUNE

"Nothing is so useless as a general maxim."

—Julia Crawford

After the death of my mother, I heard so many well-intentioned people say so many of the same things to me: Be strong, your mother would have wanted it that way. You should be thankful that she is not suffering anymore. I know how you feel, I lost my mother too. And, although I knew they meant well, I wanted to scream at them: Maybe my mother would have wanted me to cry and carry on, how do you know? While I am thankful *she* is not suffering, I can't quite get around the fact that *I* clearly am. You *don't* know what it is like, because you are you and I am I.

It might be a comfort to know that other people have suffered tragedy and loss in their lives, and moved on. But it is also a comfort to know that no one has experienced it quite like we have.

"*Your love, Lord, reaches to heaven; your truth to the skies.*"

—Psalm 35

I love to lie in the sun. I know that it is bad for me, but feeling the warmth of the sun's rays on my body is one of the nicest sensations going, if you ask me. Perhaps even more wonderful than that, though, is the feeling that can come about merely staring up at the limitless expanse of the sky. When it seems as if the pressure, struggle, and sadness of the world can crowd me in, taking a few minutes to look upward makes me aware of how small some of my problems can be, compared with the love of a God that can fill all the blue space I survey.

"The priests and elders were amazed as they observed the self-assurance of Peter and John."

—Acts of the Apostles 4:13

They could have offered all kinds of excuses, Peter and John, as to why they just couldn't perform the tasks they were chosen to perform. How can I preach, when I can barely read? How can I offer keen theological insights, when I have never formally studied? How can I make a lame man walk, when I know nothing about the healing arts? All kinds of excuses could have been made, but in the end Peter and John knew that the key was not how educated, or high-born, or even qualified they were to do what the Lord had asked of them. No, the key was their faith that God could work amazing things through them, through their weakness, through their frail humanity with all its limitations.

"How can I get through this?" we are tempted to ask ourselves from time to time. Peter and John clearly knew the answer. Do we?

4

"The apostles and elders accordingly convened to look into the matter."

—Acts of the Apostles 15:6

There can be a tendency to romanticize the Early Church at times, to wonder why things and people can't be as faith-filled as things and people were in those first couple of centuries after the death and resurrection of Jesus. Indeed, there is much we can learn from the heroic faith of these ancestors of ours.

It is also important to remember, however, that in addition to the wondrous, almost idyllic faith that was evidenced among these people, they also had to deal with dissension, controversy, confusion, and sorrow. Perhaps the real thing that separates us from them is that they knew they could not deal with it all alone, but rather relied on one another to help make sense of it.

It would behoove us to follow their lead, convening and looking into the matter.

"One ought, every day at least, to hear a little song, read a good poem, see a fine picture, and, if it were possible, to speak a few reasonable words."

—Johann Wolfgang von Goethe

My first exposure to poetry (outside of nursery rhymes) was reading Vachel Lyndsay's "The Congo" with my mother. The poem has a musicality about it, with a refrain that calls to mind tribal drums beating deep in the heart of the African jungle. What a world it opened up to me, this curious poem. What a delight it was learning the words of it myself, sharing in the drama of it, shouting out "Boomlay boomlay boom-lay boom!" and then collapsing into my mother, giggling from the excitement of it all.

That there is something about poetry, and literature, and art, and music that taps into a unique part of the human soul is beyond doubt. But I have also discovered, especially every time I now read this old familiar poem, that perhaps it can tap into the souls of those who have gone before us as well.

6

"Old and young, we are all on our last cruise."

—Robert Louis Stevenson

Saint Benedict encourages monks to keep death daily before our eyes. This is perhaps no better played out than when a monk professes solemn vows for life. The monk lies prostrate on the floor and is covered with a funeral pall. The bell ordinarily reserved for announcing the death of a monk is tolled. The cantor intones an antiphon that begins: "Now I am dead." This can all seem a bit morbid to people, and it has been known to startle visitors.

But the truth of it all remains, even if we don't like to think about it: All of us will die. And realizing this somehow makes us live better, if we pay attention to life. It also makes those who have gone before us in death not seem so remote from us, for we realize that they have gone where we will one day follow.

> *"What passion cannot music rise and quell?"*
>
> —John Dryden

One of my favorite stories as a child was *The Secret Garden*, by Frances Hodges Burnett. In the story, a bitter young girl's life is transformed through the wonders of a garden. Not too long ago, I got to see a musical version of the tale, and it only added to the beauty of it. There is perhaps no better vehicle for a story than through the wonders of music.

Even if we can't sing a note, even if we don't know Mozart from Madonna, there exists within music—from Bach to the Backstreet Boys—something that can touch us in a way that nothing, or no one else can. No one, of course, but God; whose ultimate symphony of love is the fullest expression of every note ever written.

"There is no substitute for hard work."
—Thomas Alva Edison

Work. For some the word calls to mind careers, of whatever it is that allows us to acquire the things in life that we need. For some the word calls to mind a different kind of labor, working in the garden, cleaning the house, whatever it is that allows us to get done the things that need to get done to make our surroundings more pleasing, more bearable.

Life, of course, is work, although we don't always want to think of it that way. But if we are really to acquire that which we really need (love, security, hope), and we are really to be able to make our surroundings more pleasing, more bearable (through forgiveness, healing, patience) then we must work at it. There really is no substitute.

"There is more to life than increasing its speed."

—Mahatma Gandhi

Where's the fire? Haste makes waste. Slow and steady wins the race. What's your hurry? Our language is so filled with such little aphorisms and phrases (speedily uttered, of course) that it is not difficult to draw the conclusion that many of us have a difficult time slowing down. Maybe we have too much to do, and we need to crowd as much in as we possibly can into a short span of time. Maybe the world itself revolves at a hectic pace, and we need to move quickly just to keep up. Maybe we think if we speed from one thing to another we can outrun those things such as sorrow, regret, and pain that chase after us. We should take as our model, of course, the One whose slow descent through the streets of Jerusalem and slow ascent to the wood of the cross has given the world the ultimate model of what life is really about.

"As for me, I trust in your merciful love."

—Psalm 12

I can remember thinking after my mother died that I wasn't quite sure whether I wanted to live in a world like the one I was in. I looked around and I saw three motherless children and a husband devoid of the presence of a wife, and this tempered my vision, so that I started seeing tragedy and suffering everywhere, and very little else. This was the world, and I quite frankly didn't want anything to do with it, although I knew, of course, that I would continue to have to have everything to do with it.

There are still times when I lament that the world is not what it should be. But I also see people being kind to one another, the beauty of nature, the wonders of loving relationships. And, seeing these signs all around me, I realize that the tragedies of the world do not have the final say to one who trusts in God's merciful love.

"The beautiful souls are they that are universal, open, and ready for all things."

—Montaigne

The death of a loved one can bring to birth a host of absolute statements: I'll never be truly happy again. I'll never marry again. I'll always feel alone in this world. I'll never understand why this had to happen. I'll never accept this. And while such absolutes are natural, the reality of the situation is that growth comes, not in allowing absolutes to crowd our life, but, rather, allowing possibilities instead to open up our lives. The facts remain that, even if we cannot imagine it now, we may be happy again, we may marry again, we may not always feel so alone, we may accept it all.

Loss closes off so much in our lives, makes so much ugly. Only the grace of acknowledging that possibilities exist can open our souls, and restore some of the beauty that was once there.

*"I like to walk about the beautiful
things that adorn the world."*

—George Santayana

Every evening, if the weather is pleasant enough, several of us take a walk after dinner. The purpose of the walk is never really exercise—indeed some of us have been chastised by others because we walk too fast. No, the purpose of the walk is to share a word or two with our brothers, and drink in the beauty of the rolling hills of southern Indiana. We never really have anywhere to *go*, so the destination is unimportant; the journey, however is.

It is just such a notion that is the foundation of the notion of pilgrimage, even the pilgrimage known as life itself. In so worrying about getting from Point A to Point B, or completely bypassing Point A or Point B because we don't like the scenery, we lose sight of the sheer importance of the trip, where much is discovered about ourselves, about others, and about God.

"Shared joy is double joy, and shared sorrow is half sorrow."

—Swedish proverb

There are those who would say that you shouldn't complain about the hand that life has dealt you; no one likes a whiner—get over it. There are those who say if you are blessed with great fortune that you shouldn't advertise it; no one likes a braggart—keep it to yourself. People who say this seem to be missing the point. We are all connected on this planet, and my joys and sorrows affect you, just as your joys and sorrows affect me. We can no more make sense of the dreams and delights, the tragedies and terrors of life by ourselves than we can hope to simultaneously sing all the parts of Handel's *Messiah* alone.

14

"I will be their God, and they shall be my people."

—Jeremiah 31:33

My grandmother made the best cinnamon rolls in the world. Soft bread, sticky cinnamon (especially in the middle) rich, thick icing: eating one of these rolls was a connection to the best the world had to offer—sweetness, warmth, satisfaction.

I know now that the rolls were also a connection to Grandma, indeed to my entire family. Because besides the amazing ingredients that went into them, Grandma put love, and stories, and life in them. And again and again I was able to taste of this connection, to savor life's sweetness. And even though Grams is no longer here, every time I taste a bit of cinnamon, a bit of icing, I am able to have a little taste of her love, which was for me the best the world had to offer—sweetness, warmth, satisfaction.

"Fear is useless. What is needed is trust."

—Mark 5:36

Once, as a small boy, I remember being awakened in the middle of the night by a great deal of activity outside my bedroom door. My mother was sick, and an ambulance was there to take her to the hospital. Every night after this event I had terrible dreams, and I would wake up nearly paralyzed with fear, my very joints aching. Inevitably, I would make my way to my parents' room, where my father would try to console me and put my fears to rest so that I could rest. My worrying was not going to make anything better, he would tell me. It wasn't the best explanation, but it worked at the time.

Many people face fear of one kind or another on a daily basis. In the midst of this Jesus tells us to replace our useless fear with trust. It is perhaps not the best explanation, but if we really do trust, it just might work.

"Live on in my love."

—John 15:9

The resiliency of the human being is astounding. We live a life of constant change, of frequent struggle, of inestimable happiness. Indeed it is not uncommon for all of these things to happen in our lives in relatively short time periods. And through it all, we somehow manage to move on, to keep trudging through a world that is fast paced, wonderful, and not just a little confusing.

How do we manage? What is it that enables us to take such a variety of experiences and make sense of them? What is it that enables us not to be done in by what can at times seem like the sheer enormity of a life lived to its fullest?

Some would say it's a mystery, and they're right, although not perhaps in the way that they think. It *is* a mystery. It is *the* mystery of God's passionate love for us.

"Man needs to suffer. Griefs purify and prepare him."

— José Martí

Anyone who regularly watches the evening news cannot fail but be mindful of the suffering in the world: natural disasters, violence, civil strife, hatred, immoral politicians—the list of the world's woes goes on and on. When you combine them with the personal woes that we and others experience, watching the evening news can become like swallowing bitter medicine, and we can begin to wonder if the price of being informed is worth the pain.

But then, every once in a while, a story will come on about a family who lost everything but still managed to put their child through Harvard by selling handmade doormats and you realize that it indeed is all worth it, that the pain doesn't always have the final say.

18

"*This time, like all times, is a very good one, if we but know what to do with it.*"

—Ralph Waldo Emerson

We learn as children, it seems, the ability to wish for a future time to be upon us. I wish I were old enough to stay up late. I wish I were sixteen so I could drive. I wish I were in college so that I could be on my own. I wish I had more seniority at work so that I could have more vacation time. I wish I was on vacation. And, perhaps most deeply: I wish this hurt was over.

Wishing for a future removed from whatever situation might be a natural thing to do, but it is clearly not the best thing to do. Because—if we accept the grace that is around us—we can learn so much from what is going on in our lives right here and right now, and so better bring about a time when the hurt really is over.

"I will give you a new heart and place a new spirit within you, taking from your bodies your stony hearts and giving you natural hearts."

—Ezekiel 36:26

I once visited in the hospital a woman whose husband and son had perished in a fire that nearly claimed her own life. As soon as I walked into the room, she screamed at me to leave. "I don't want anything to do with God!" she cried in anguish, her obvious pain causing me to wince. I left, and the nurses told me not to come back.

But I think about her often. Part of me wonders if her suffering did her in, if she is no longer able to live and love because of the sheer tragedy of what she had to endure. You can't really blame her, on one level, for hardening her heart against God: it *is* all a bit too much.

Another part of me wonders—indeed, hopes—that a heart naturally hardened by such suffering could somehow be softened by a God who is also a bit too much.

20

"*Yes, Virginia, there is a Santa Claus.*"

—Francis Pharcellus Church

It never dawned on me as a child how unlikely it all was, this Santa Claus business. That one man could somehow keep track of everyone who was naughty, and everyone who was nice was astounding enough, but in addition to all of this he was somehow able to get to every single home in the world and deliver gifts in the span of a single night. Ignorance of the intricacies of intercontinental travel aside, one would have thought that I would have maybe been able to figure it out, but I didn't. You see, I wanted to believe, and the power of belief is a formidable entity indeed.

Jesus promised that whoever believed in Him would never die. If I could for so long believe in Santa Claus, who is a myth, then how much more powerful should the effects of my belief in the very real words of Jesus be.

"I will entrust you the keys of the kingdom of heaven."

—Matthew 16:19

Brother Methodius was an odd little man, or at least I remember him that way. A man of few words, he limped—shuffled, really—around, whistling a tune I could never make out, keeping time by slapping his hand against the side of his leg. But for all his quirks, I once heard him described as the most powerful man here, because, being the locksmith, he could open absolutely any door in this institution. There is definitely a power in possessing keys.

Imagine the power involved in being given the keys to the kingdom of heaven. And although this power was given to Peter and his successors, we have a share in that power, whenever we seek to open doors closed to sadness and struggle, seeing the promise that lies beyond. Imagine what life could be like, if we opened such doors.

"Love bade me welcome: yet my soul drew back, Guilty of dust and sin."

—George Herbert

Peoples' notion of sin often falls into two opposing camps: some people seem to see sin everywhere, while others wouldn't know a sin (or at least acknowledge it) if it came up and bit them on the nose. The healthiest stance is in the middle somewhere, as the healthiest stance often is. We need to be patient with ourselves and others, and realize that we and they are human, and prone to fail from time to time. And yet we also must make sure that we acknowledge those times when we have consciously chosen something that we know is not right, and hold ourselves accountable. In recognizing that which is mere human frailty as well as that which is just plain wrong, we begin to free ourselves from past hurts and fears, making room for Love.

"Their eyes, mid many wrinkles, their eyes, / Their ancient, glittering eyes are gay."

—William Butler Yeats

She was always larger than life to me: big fleshy arms, hands that could squeeze my face so hard that I feared the indentations would be permanent; major laughing and crying—in both instances her dark eyes a troubadour of life's wonders. She had a nasty side (who doesn't) but I never saw it, only heard about it. Instead I only experienced an enormous love that rushed right out of her big heart, through her eyes, to my eyes, resting in my heart.

As my grandmother lay dying, now small and frail, I was struck deep within that heart by the sense of loss of someone so grand to me, a loss that seemed to grow larger as her body grew smaller yet. But a couple of times, the last time I saw her, her eyes opened briefly, and I caught just a glimpse of that big love, and I realized it was still there somehow, being far too big to go away.

24

*"A leper approached Jesus with a
request: 'If you will to do so, you can
cure me.' Moved with pity, Jesus
stretched out his hand, touched him,
and said: 'I do will it. Be cured.'"*

—Mark 1:40-41

He wants the same for us, of course.
Aware of how we struggle, mindful
of that within us which needs healing,
moved with pity for us, He wants us to be
cured as well. He desires not that sorrow
and suffering should have the final say in
our lives, but joy and life. He desires that
the darkness which can so surround us at
times be vanquished by the inestimable
brilliance of His light. He wills all of this
for us, so great is His love.

We need only stretch out our hand
to Him to be cured.

"One must not always think so much about what one should do, but rather what one should be."

—Meister Eckhart

"What do you do?" On a recent trip, I encountered all kinds of adults who asked me that question. Part of the questioning, I'm sure, comes from a natural curiosity about monks—people worry that we sit and pray all day. But part of it comes from our society's emphasis on our worth coming from what we do. I pray. I write. I sing. I administrate.

In contrast to this is what children asked me: What's your favorite color? Do you like vegetables? Who's your favorite basketball player? The answers to these questions ultimately had more to do with who I am than those asked by their parents.

This is yet another example of how we should be childlike. God loves and helps us because of who we *are*, not what we *do*.

"So they said to him, "Then what sign do you do, that we may see, and believe in you?"

—John 24:30

They had listened spellbound as he preached God's kingdom of love, His words combining like a beautiful symphony. They had seen Him extend his hands in loving touch, bringing healing and solace to people who needed His presence, His touch to go on living. They had seen Him take five loaves and two fishes, and from that feed thousands of people. And still, after all this, they wanted a sign.

We're not too different from these people, because we too long for signs. And like these people, the signs are in our midst: in the gentle fall of spring rain, the anguished cry of a sorrowing mother, in the tender caress of lovers. Yes, signs of God's care for us are all around us, but all too often we are so preoccupied looking for the signs we *think* we should see, that we miss the ones that are right in front of us.

"And when he came out of the boat, there met him out of the tombs a man with an unclean spirit."

—Mark 5:2

Of all the people in need of Jesus' healing in the gospels, perhaps none is as tragic as the Gerasene demoniac, whose life was lived in darkness and desperation, shackled to the harsh coldness of the tombs, bruising himself with stones, crying out in anguish against the demons that so plagued him.

We, in perhaps different ways, face our demons too: demons of fear, loss, regret, anger. And there are times, when in despair, we can allow these demons to keep us shackled to fear, hurting ourselves with the stones of regret, crying out in the anguish of loss. But if we accept the healing touch of our God, so often manifested through caring people, then we can begin to see the place of warmth, light and love that will allow us to flee far from our demons, far from our tombs.

*"You need patience to do God's will
and receive what he has promised."*
—Hebrews 10:36

Patience, so they say, is a virtue. And of all the virtues out there, perhaps it is the most difficult for many of us. We live in a world where many things are instant, and having to wait for something, not being able to *do* anything about it, can be unnerving. We want what we want now.

And so it is that we can be impatient, even with the way we grieve. Why does this continue to affect me so? Why can't I feel better about this sooner? Faith, of course, is the only antidote to poisonous impatience. Faith that God will deliver what has been promised. And faith that God will take care of things on God's time, not necessarily ours.

"O Lord, you search me and you know me, you know my resting and my rising, you discern my purpose from afar."
—Psalm 138

When, as a freshman in college, I went away from home for the first extended time, I talked to my father a great deal on the phone. The mere presence of Dad's voice on the phone could cheer me up, assure me that financial help was on the way, give me sympathy when I needed it, and—perhaps more frequently with a college freshman—give me a kick in the pants when I needed that too. My father seemingly had the ability to be able to tell how I felt and what I needed by simply listening to my voice, and even if there were things that I felt I wanted to hide from him, he ultimately ferreted them out of me.

So it is with God. The presence of our God can cheer us up, assure us that help is on the way, give us sympathy, and give us a kick in the pants when we need it. We need only call on Him.

"My soul is like this cloudy, opal ring."
—Arthur Symons

There have been times in my life when I have been awash with sheer joy, and my soul seemed to soar in brilliant light to the source of all light. There have been times in my life when I have been weighted down by sorrow, and my soul seemed to be buried deep in the darkness. There have been times when I have fallen, not lived up to my potential, and my soul was wounded, and needing healing. And when I reflect on it all, I realize that the state of my soul has been different from one time to another, but that its beauty—a beauty made manifest because of my connection to God—is never in doubt, and, like a ring, is somehow eternal, and, like an opal, is captivating even in its cloudiness.

JULY

"By means of many such parables he taught them the message in a way they could understand."

—Mark 4:33

Hypostatic union. Homousias. Transignification. People who make it their business to study theology have all kinds of words to help get across ideas that are enormous in their implications, as broad as the very sky. And it's good to study these things, to expand our minds to the possibilities that exist in our God.

But, when faced with all-too-human struggles, ultimately it is not so much these things that comfort us most, but simple stories of hope and love Jesus told that—if we let them—can touch our hearts in ways that nothing else can. Let us never neglect entering into these stories, for they are the best ways to teach us of God's love in a way we can understand.

2

"*My God, my God, why have you for-saken me?*"

—Psalm 21

The last time I was home I went to the cemetery where my grandparents are buried. The wind was blowing fiercely over the prairie of central Illinois, and a mournful howling was in the air all around me. I stood before their grave, and remembered my grandmother's big arms around me, my grandfather whistling and playing cards, and at that moment—regardless of the fact that I was just about a mile from scores of relatives—I felt so terribly alone in the world that tears seemed to be the only way I could give voice to the emptiness.

To be human is to know, at one time or another, loneliness. And, although it doesn't make the loneliness easier, it is good for us to realize that every time we feel forsaken, we are participating in that moment when one man was visible alone and suffering against a blood red sky.

"'If I just touch his clothing,' she thought, 'I shall get well.'"

—Mark 5:28

I have a couple of books of my mother's lesson plans from her teaching days, and I love to get them out and look at them every now and then. Seeing her handwriting, wondering what she talked about when she had written "current events," imagining what she did with her free period makes her seem a little more real, a little more present than she ordinarily seems.

Many people don't understand the practice of venerating relics, those bones and other things connected to saints. I have often heard it referred to as morbid, strange. And maybe, in some instances, it is. But maybe in other instances it is our natural way of trying to make sure that a connection is not lost. Maybe it is our way of touching something and getting well.

4

"We have been much consoled by your faith throughout our distress and trial."
—1 Thessalonians 3:7-8

I recently talked with a young woman whose father has been diagnosed with a terminal illness. I told her—quite sincerely—that I would be praying for him and the whole family. She seemed as if maybe she was getting tired of hearing this, said she wasn't sure what it meant for people to be praying. What did it do?

I had no answer for her. I could only tell her that, even if I didn't understand how it all worked on God's end, there could be a real strength and comfort in knowing that people were remembering us. Knowing that, as we struggle and try to make sense out of it all, others are in some way sharing in that struggle, can make a difference. Even if it doesn't seem that God is helping much through our prayers, we need to know that we are helping each other. And of course, when we help each other, God is, in the end, helping us after all.

"Gigantic, willful, young, Chicago sitteth at the northwest gates."
—William Vaughn Moody

One evening years ago my friend Steve and I went to a wonderful play at the Schubert Theatre in my favorite city, Chicago. Afterwards we walked in the delightful weather of a perfect spring night to a nearby restaurant where we spent hours talking religion and literature, at the end even bringing our waitress in on the lively discussion. We then walked to Lake Michigan, the waves crashing against the giant rocks, soaking us as we squealed with laughter. It was a perfect night in a fantastic city with a wonderful friend.

I don't get to Chicago too often these days, and, regrettably, I don't see Steve as much as I would like. But every now and then, in the midst of daily traumas, I'll close my eyes and savor this memory. And Steve is somehow here, as is Chicago and its arrogant lake.

6

"As he walked by the Sea of Galilee, he saw two brothers, Simon, who is called Peter, and Andrew, his brother, casting a net into the sea. They were fishermen."

—Matthew 4:18

There is an extreme comfort in knowledge of the fact that the Lord chose such ordinary people to be His Apostles. Because if He could take someone as wishy-washy as Peter, or as shifty as Matthew, or as impetuous as James and John and raise them to a new level, then we can hope that He can take us—ordinary people that we are—and raise us to new levels as well. We can have faith that, even if we are currently sinking in the depths of an ocean of despair, the Lord's net is quite capable of snaring us and bringing us up to the light of the sun.

"He made a kind of whip of cords and drove them all out of the temple area, sheep and oxen alike, and knocked over the money-changers' tables, spilling their coins."

—John 2:13-15

The anger that is a result of missed opportunities, wounded pride, or hurt feelings can be intense, but, more often than not, it can subside quickly. Not so with the anger that comes from disappointment—in others, in ourselves, in the circumstances of life. I think it is just such anger that Jesus exhibited in the temple, and it is often the anger that can accompany the loss of a loved one. We are disappointed, and this disappointment gives way to questioning which can give way to anger. Like Jesus, it seems to me that a worthwhile endeavor is to find a way that we can express this anger that we have within us, even if it is directed at Him.

"Friend and neighbor you have taken away: my one companion is darkness."

—Psalm 87

"All my friends are dead," a 93 year-old woman once told me, and, though I was only 27 at the time, her words touched upon something in me as well. I think there are times when an innate loneliness can strike us, make us aware that, although we may be surrounded by a plethora of friends and loved ones, there are still times when we are asked to make part of our journey seemingly alone, in the dark, far from the enlightening presence of those whom we hold dear.

Many saints throughout the ages could tell us, however, that the darkness is not an absence of something, but rather is filled with a presence beyond all our imagining. In this sense—the sense of faith—we begin to see just what a companion darkness can be.

"To make a prairie it takes a clover and one bee, / One clover, and a bee, / And revery."

—Emily Dickinson

How to begin again. How to take what was unimaginable, imagine it, realize it, and somehow move forward. How to so change our hearts that the sadness that we feel there like a thorn can be rendered less sharp, and give way to the rose of healing, fragrant with love. How to begin again.

We begin again by small steps. We move forward delicately, like a bee hovering near a fragile flower stem. We change our hearts by allowing glimpses of happiness to bloom there. We begin again, by praying for the grace that the love which never dies will never die in us, will always sustain us with its delightful fragrance.

10

"The earth quaked, boulders split, tombs opened."

—Matthew 26:51-52

Upon entering the Archabbey Church, one can't help but notice the giant Christus, or image of Christ, that soars from behind the organ pipes in the apse. He looks a bit stern, standing there in flowing royal robes, His long, bony fingers pointing to a book that He is holding bearing the words: Ego Sum Vita— I am the Life. It is a definitive, no-nonsense, powerful Jesus Christ that we see.

It seems there has been a tendency in recent years to emphasize the humanity of Jesus, stress just how like us He really was. And, although this is clearly of great spiritual benefit, I can't help but take great comfort in the image depicted in our church. Because though I can take comfort in one who suffered, I also delight in one powerful enough to overcome it.

"*On the evening of the first day of the week, even though the disciples had locked the doors of the place where they were for fear of the authorities….*"

—John 20:19

It seems to me they had good reason to be afraid, these disciples of Jesus. Just imagine the thoughts that had to be running through their minds in regard to what they had witnessed: Jesus, supposedly the all-powerful messiah, stooping down and washing feet. Frightening. Jesus, the one to conquer their foes and establish a reign of peace, Himself conquered and beaten by brutal violence. Frightening. Jesus, the way, the truth, and the life, stripped of life. Frightening. And add to all of that also that many of the people in Jerusalem were hostile to them, and that upon visiting the tomb the body was not where it should be, they indeed had good reason to be gathered in fear, to be frightened. Fear, after all, although not ideal, is definitely understandable, definitely human.

"We boil at different degrees."

—Ralph Waldo Emerson

I recently talked to a friend who attended the funeral of another friend for which I was unable to be present, and the one thing that kept coming up over and over again was the fact that the deceased man's wife didn't shed a tear. My friend was upset by this; how could she not be moved when her husband was now gone? It seemed, to him, uncaring, a bit cold.

I assured him that there is no standard to grief. The person who weeps violently and throws himself on a grave isn't necessarily grieving any more than the person who quietly stands by; it's just that how one person handles it, expresses it, is different from the other.

"He said to them again, 'Do you still not understand?'"

—Mark 8:21

It is hard for us to imagine how we would have viewed Jesus had we walked the earth with Him like His disciples did. We may be prone to think that if we had witnessed Him feeding four or five thousand with just a few loaves and fishes, that we would probably get the picture a little quicker than some of them did. Could they not see what He did for them?

Of course, we need ask the question of ourselves as well: can we not see what He does for us? When our vision becomes clouded due to loss, it is important for us to remember that everything we have comes from God, through Jesus. And so we are surrounded by His manifestations. Do we still not understand?

"We be of one blood, ye and I."

—Rudyard Kipling

Last summer I spent a few weeks studying Gregorian chant at the Abbey of Solesmes in France. The monks there are known for their chant, and the strict formality of their services. I was a nervous wreck, each day a struggle trying to figure out which book to use for which service, which utensil to use at dinner, my mind swimming with Latin and French. Fortunately, next to me in choir and at table was a young monk named Frère Bruno, who patiently helped me find my place. In the silence of the monastery I would merely look at him, my eyes singing gratitude, his eyes replying (in Latin chant, of course) somehow that he understood.

I am becoming more and more certain that there are no strangers in the world, and the intense connection of all humanity can be a strength for us all.

"When he got to the house, the blind men caught up with him. Jesus said to them, 'Are you confident I can do this?' 'Yes, Lord,' they told him."

—Matthew 9:28

If only this faith business were easier, we can sometimes think. We are expected to have faith in the working of a God whom it is so difficult to see and hear. We are expected to have faith that eventually the just are rewarded and the sinful repaid, even when we can see all kinds of examples of just the opposite. We are expected to have faith that we will somehow be able to rise above the traumas of our lives, even when it seems that we are sinking fast. If only this faith business were easier, we can sometimes think.

It seems pretty easy for the two blind men. They looked to nowhere and no one but Jesus to get what they so desperately needed, and then they got what they so desperately needed. Are you confident that I can do this? We are. What could be easier?

16

"And there is even a happiness / That makes the heart afraid."

—Thomas Hood

I don't remember when first I laughed after the death of my mother. Memories of tears and anger and confusion come readily, but the memory of that first laugh, where the light somehow broke through the darkness around me is lost, although I know it occurred sooner or later. I remember for so long after her death, walking around, feeling that I could not partake in so many of the pursuits that had been the joy of my childhood: baseball, basketball, swimming, bike riding, tag, hide and seek. To give into these, to truly enjoy life again I felt would be a betrayal of who I was, and what I felt, even of her memory. But then, the laughter came, although I do not remember when, and with its first infectious sound I realized that it was not a betrayal of anything, but a recognition of the healing that so needed to happen in my life.

"Ask, and you will receive."

—Matthew 7:7

The impracticality of owning a horse while living in town never really dawned on me, and because of it I asked for one over and over again. We had a big back yard, I figured, and—standard kid line—I would feed it and water it and wash it and you won't even know it's there. Of course, my father didn't go in for the whole horse idea—having the ability to see the bigger picture that escaped me—and so I never got one.

When Jesus says ask and you will receive, it is easy for us to point to all kinds of things that we have asked for from Him and apparently never received. Of course, we need to trust that Jesus has the ability to see the bigger picture, and can help us to ask the right questions.

17

J
U
L
Y

18

"*My brothers, what good is it to profess faith without practicing it?*"

—James 2:14

We can say that we desire, with Christ, that all be one, but until we tear down the barriers that exist between us our words don't mean a whole lot. We can say, with Christ, that whatever we do to one of the lowly ones, we do to Him, but if we don't help the lowly ones our words don't mean a whole lot. We can say, with Christ, that whosoever believes in Him shall not die, but have eternal life, but if we allow death to have the final say over us our words don't mean a whole lot.

Mourning and questioning go hand in hand, and lamenting our loss with words of confusion and pain does not go against our faith, but can be a manifestation of grappling with that faith. But if for one moment we think that death has won, we're clearly not practicing our faith.

"'And you,' he went on to ask, *'who do you say that I am?'"*

—Mark 8:29

You are at times my greatest frustration and other times my greatest joy. You are one who at times seems to want me to suffer and at other times wants to free me from suffering. You are one who at times seems to be more serious than I ever hope to be, and at other times seems to be a regular Henny Youngman. You are the one who at times brings me such life, but at other times makes me wonder if you'll be the death of me. And maybe that's the ultimate joke, the ultimate zinger: if I let you be the death of me, you most certainly will be my life. Take my life. Please.

"*Rising early the next morning, he went off to a lonely place in the desert; there he was absorbed in prayer.*"

—Mark 1:35

Life seems to move much more quickly than it used to, and we are becoming masters at cutting back where we need to so that we can fit more in. The world spins at a much faster pace, they say, and you need to keep up or you'll get left behind. A stitch in time saves nine. The list of speedy aphorisms goes on and on.

I would like to add a different one: If you cut too many corners the piece disappears. In running from event to event, we can run away from that which we really need to face. It's a risk, therefore, to slow down, to face it all, and to listen for God's voice telling us what to do. The answer might be too slow in coming for our tastes, and we might not like what we hear, but ultimately if we can try to absorb ourselves in prayer like the Lord did, then maybe we can begin to see meaning in our life as He did in his.

> *"Summer afternoon—summer afternoon; to me those have always been the two most beautiful words in the English language."*
>
> —Henry James

It was a time when the hardest decision was whether to swim or to play ball. It was a time when shoes were clearly not needed to go the places I wanted to go. It was a time that, even if it rained, the weather was just perfect for whatever it was I wanted to do. It was a time when I didn't have to *do* anything, if I didn't want to. It was a time—the typical summer afternoon of my youth—when life seemed simpler, more beautiful, and much more hope-filled than it does now.

But memory has the ability to make us long for better times, often not giving thought to the other events of some summer afternoons: the tears, the loneliness. Looking at the whole picture, we begin to realize that the wonders of summer afternoon, the excitement of a world that holds so much possibility— all of this is still with us, regardless of how many winters have followed.

22

*"A man came up to Jesus and said,
'Teacher, what good must I do to
possess everlasting life?"*

—Matthew 19:16

He knew what questions to ask.
Encountering Jesus, the wonder-
worker, the man could presumably have
asked anything, and I have to imagine
there were some questions posed to Jesus
that didn't make it into the gospel
accounts that were less than stirring in
their depth. But this man knew what
questions to ask, and so he came to Jesus,
the Answer, with the important queries of
eternity perched on his lips, curled in confusion and doubt, wonder and revelation.

When so much in our lives can be
tempered by loss, we must realize that
we, too, need to know what questions to
ask, and come to Jesus, the Answer. We
might not always like what we find out,
and the manner of lesson might be
harsh, but we can rest assured that if we
truly listen to Him we'll find out all that
we need to know: the confusion and
doubt, the wonder and revelation.

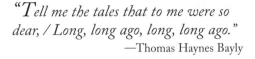

"Tell me the tales that to me were so dear, / Long, long ago, long, long ago."
—Thomas Haynes Bayly

As I grew older and memories of my mother began to fade, I began asking people who knew her well to tell stories about her. Any story that anyone could tell would be welcomed by me, regardless of how seemingly boring or banal it may have appeared. I realized from an early age that memories and stories were linked to life itself, and if life was to continue in some way—especially my mother's life—there was no other way for it to do so than to talk about her, think about her, listen about her.

Some people seem to think that there comes a time to move on from grief, to stop bringing up old pain; and to some extent they may be right. But we must never allow ourselves to move on completely, for life (and its story) is too important.

"*They kept this word of his to themselves, though they continued to discuss what 'to rise from the dead' meant.*"

—Mark 9:10

Here were Peter, James, and John. They had just witnessed the transfiguration of Jesus, seeing Him decked in brilliance, cavorting with the likes of Moses and Elijah, and, even after such an elaborate display of divinity, they still had a few questions, primary among them being, "What does it mean to rise from the dead?" They didn't have all the answers, and they needed to talk about it all to try to make sense of the wonderful confusion that swirled throughout their lives.

We're not different. We are told that when we die we are raised to new life with Jesus. It in no way is a reflection of a weak faith to wonder exactly how all of that works; it is, indeed, quite the contrary.

> *"Even after a bad harvest, there must be sowing."*
>
> —Seneca

The other evening, in the middle of singing Sunday Vespers, the sung service that finishes our celebration of Sunday with due solemnity, the organ quit, ceasing to put forth its melodious accompaniment with a bang and a whimper. All eyes turned to the helpless organist, who shrugged his shoulders, giving a clear signal to the community that there was absolutely nothing he could do, just keep singing. And singing we did, without missing a beat.

After vespers had ended, I reflected on what a great analogy for life itself the whole experience was. Because there are going to be all kinds of difficulties that could easily stop us in our tracks, if we let them. And though it may be tempting to shut down, to just stop, the real grace comes our way when—somehow—we allow the music to continue through us.

"Simon and his companions managed to track him down, and when they found him, they told him, 'Everybody is looking for you!'"

—Mark 1:36-37

I used to think that Simon's statement was a bit of an exaggeration. There were so many people in Jesus' day who couldn't have cared less what this strange preacher was up to. There had to have been people who were less than interested in hearing about seeds and yeast, about wedding banquets and long-lost children.

The more I experience human nature, however, I think that it is not so much of an exaggeration after all. Because we all sense emptiness in lives from time to time. We all seek words of comfort and love, of assurance. And when we find ourselves wanting such things, looking for such things, we are looking for Him. Because He's the only one who can fill the emptiness, who can speak the words we need to hear.

"Nothing that was worthy in the past departs; no truth or goodness realized by man ever dies, or can die."

—Thomas Carlyle

I was about 16 years old when my grandmother said to me, "Your mother will never be dead as long as you are alive." The context was not as soft and emotional as it sounds, as her catalyst for saying it was her observation of me butting my way into various conversations, stirring up trouble, and then moving on. But even still, I loved hearing it. I loved that even nine years after her death someone was able to make a connection between the two of us. I loved the thought that there was something in me that her own mother recognized as something that was in her as well.

We all carry around traits, quirks, looks, habits—you name it—that those who have gone before have carried around as well. Recognizing them, celebrating them makes our connection to them seem as real as it is, as well as making death seem less final somehow.

*"More things are wrought by prayer /
Than this world dreams of."*
—Alfred, Lord Tennyson

In this very practical world of ours that measures success by output, I am often called upon to defend the monastic life. "What do you guys do there, just pray all the time?" is a common question, and no matter how much I talk about the work we do here, people can't seem to understand why we would gather in church four times a day, every day. "How can you get anything done, going to church so much?"

I can't measure out for these people what exactly all that prayer has wrought. I can't point to something specific that has been changed in the world because of it, although I have my suspicions about a thing or two. But I can point to myself and others who somehow see the value in prayer: if it can change people like us, I have no doubt that it can change just about anything.

"The nurse of full-grown souls is solitude."

—James Russell Lowell

There can be a tendency, when our souls are aching from loss, to surround ourselves with people. It's as if we constantly have people around us, we just might not notice the emptiness that loss brings, we might think the loneliness will not seem so lonely. And while our family and friends can be enormously helpful to us, they, in the end, cannot completely fill the void. It is only in a combination of human interaction and being alone with God that we begin to heal. The silence of solitude, though sometimes bitter to swallow, is a necessary medicine for all of us.

30

"[Jesus] said to him 'Ephphatha!' (that is, 'Be opened!'). At once the man's ears were opened, he was freed from the impediment, and began to speak freely."

—Mark 7:34-35

"**B**e opened!" This is wonderful advice, not just for the poor man who couldn't hear or speak well, but for all of us, whatever our infirmity. Because to be closed is to stop living. To be closed to love, to hope, to memories, to new ways of doing things out of fear or regret or hopelessness is to be like a musician content to merely play the same piece over and over again.

Be opened, the Lord says. Be opened to love around you, even if it can seem fleeting. Be open to hope, even when feeling despair. Be open to memories, even when they can be painful. Be open to new ways of doing things, even if it's hard to let go of the old ways. In thus being opened, we find that the tune can change from the boring music of inertia to the glorious symphony of the love of God.

"There is in God, some say, a deep but dazzling darkness."

—Henry Vaughan

Many of the greatest mystics in the Christian tradition, those who through their prayer have been able to achieve a particularly intense closeness with God, have also experienced a silence, a darkness, an apparent lack of communication that can be nearly crippling. If we are supposed to pattern our life with our relationship to God in mind, then what does that pattern look like when we are having trouble relating, when we wonder if God is there at all?

The answer is to realize that in silence God can speak more eloquently and beautifully than ten thousand angels' choirs. In the darkness God's face can be seen to be more dazzling than ten thousand stars. We need not worry about silence and darkness if we realize that God can be silent and dark.

AUGUST

> *"Every parting gives a foretaste of death; every coming together again a foretaste of the resurrection."*
>
> —Arthur Schopenhauer

The day before I left for college, I went over to my grandparents' house to say goodbye. My grandmother cried (as I knew she would) and from the sheer amount of tears one would have thought that I was studying overseas, rather than a mere hour and a half away. At Thanksgiving break, my Grams smothered me with kisses and, once again, tears, and sat listening attentively as I regaled her with tales of college life (or some of it, anyway).

Four years later it was my turn to cry as her casket was placed on her grave. I knew my tears for her were somehow related to hers for me when I went away to college. I recognized also, in that way that things sometimes seem balanced in the universe, that our eventual reunion would be just as sweet, both of us smothered in a love that cannot die.

2

"*See how tiny the spark is that sets a huge forest ablaze!*"

—James 3:5

It's that first step. It's laughing at a shared joke, even when nothing but tears have preceded it. It's leaving the house to go out, even when you don't want to see another person. It's facing the routine of bills, shopping, errands, even when all of those things seem alien and overwhelming. Whatever the circumstance, it is that first step wherein a world shattered by loss is, for a moment, allowed to coexist with a world as ordinary as it's ever been. And in being able to take this first step, no matter how seemingly insignificant, we begin to see that life goes on, even if we can't fathom how. With this first step, that which is cold in us begins to feel a taste of the warmth of the healing fire of God's love.

> *"God is and all is well."*
> —John Greenleaf Whittier

Once I was driving Archabbot Lambert to a meeting that was of some importance for him. It dawned on me—forty miles out and in the midst of horrendous traffic—that there was absolutely no way that we could arrive on time, indeed we would probably be nearly an hour late. My mind kept imagining an enormous board room, with hordes of business-suited people sitting around a table, tapping pencils on the table and looking at their watches. I was a nervous wreck, and it wasn't even my meeting.

In the midst of what I clearly saw to be a trauma, the Archabbot announced to me that he was going to take a nap for a few minutes. And he did, amazingly enough. And it dawned on me how much easier life would be if I didn't spend so much energy fretting about the things I cannot change.

"Draw close to God, and he will draw close to you."

—James 4:8

We lament the distance of time, remembering moments in our lives when we were happier, and current struggles only seem to make that distance greater. We lament the distance that exists between friends and loved ones, as life's roads have taken people in different directions. We lament the distance between who we are and who we long to be, realizing with regret just how often we fall short of the mark. And in all of these distances there is an emptiness, a longing to have something filled.

We sometimes think that there is an enormous distance between God and us. When we sense this distance, we need to realize that our God is often expressed in a paradox: through silence we hear God's voice, through darkness we experience God's light, through emptiness we are filled with His presence.

"What an unbelieving lot you are!
How long must I remain with you?"
—Mark 9:19

They were a good-intentioned lot, the disciples, but even the best of people can bring about exasperation, as is clearly evidenced in the Lord's outburst to them. The disciples' inability to see the whole picture was a constant issue that Jesus had to face over and over again, and even though wondering how long He would have to stick with them is perhaps not the epitome of patience, He nonetheless was always able to stick with them.

There are good-intentioned people in our lives who, sometimes, just don't manage to see the big picture. There are people who want what is best for us, but manage to say and do the wrong things over and over again. Our impatience with them can be understandable, but we need to make it our prayer that we can always be able to stick with them.

"Many strokes overthrow the tallest oaks."

—John Lyly

When I was growing up, my father was a stickler for making sure we had our napkins on our laps at every meal. It's not that we were a particularly formal family but for some reason the napkin-on-the-lap thing was a non-negotiable, as if by making us do it my father was at least trying to get us thinking in terms of manners and other things of bigger importance.

Sometimes the small gestures we make in life often possess a relevance and importance that we only come to realize later. So we must be confident that any step we can make in the direction we need to go is the right step to make, and eventually it gets us where we're going. I am aware of this every time I pull out of a fast food drive-through, making sure my napkin is on my lap before I get on the road.

"*Next to theology, I give music the highest place and honor.*"

—Martin Luther

Every year on Palm Sunday, our schola (choir) sings a three-part, a capella version of the Passion of Jesus Christ, written by our Father Columba. It is wondrous, and the complexity of emotions surrounding the tragic story not only is played out in the text, but in the style and tone of the music as well. The notes that surround us paint such a vivid picture of that day so long ago that it is as if we're there, each crescendo a swell in the anger of the crowd, each simple softness an echo of the voice of a dying man.

There are times when I can't put into words how I am feeling, the entanglement of emotions is so rich. At those times, I turn to music, realizing that even if I can't find a voice for something, someone else may already have.

8

"Yes, God so loved the world that he gave his only Son, that whoever believes in him may not die but may have eternal life."

—John 3:16

He was, for a time, ubiquitous at sporting events, a ballpark Kilroy, always there: Sporting a rainbow wig, running around to be in front of the camera, holding a large sign that simply read: "John 3:16." How ridiculous he seemed to me, I who like my religious displays in church, preferably with organ music and incense. Indeed, my friends and I used to mock him, come up with alternative signs that we would carry around if we got the chance. We were, quite simply, embarrassed for him.

Maybe that's what he wanted. Because his sign, if nothing else, points to the embarrassing excess of a God for whom death can be an instrument of love. How divinely ridiculous.

"By means of many such parables he taught them the message in a way they could understand."

—Mark 4:33

My friend Phil and I both graduated from small, Midwestern high schools in 1984, so our conversations are filled with allusions to the movies, videos, music, and trends that marked those years of big hair and parachute pants. Although we now lead very different lives (he's married with children and I'm a monk) we nevertheless often seem to find common ground because we share the same vocabulary.

Jesus often told stories to His listeners in language that was clearly going to make sense to them, so earnest was His desire to help them know of the wondrous, confusing love of God. That He used stories of vineyards and seeds where we may rely on references to Brady Bunch episodes isn't as important as the fact that we continue to teach each other the message in ways that we all understand.

"O that I had wings like a dove to fly away and be at rest."

—Psalm 54

How attractive a thought, when mired down by the very real sorrows and struggles of life, to imagine soaring above it all. How calming to envision a whole new perspective from up there, where the problems down below don't affect us, where everything seems small, where nothing can touch us. And though the tendency to want to get away from it all is natural, and escape can even be good, even doves must eventually land back on the earth, their peaceful cooing expressed in the midst of the more harsh music of life's struggles.

The wonder is, I think, not that they can fly above it all, but rather that they can continue to make such sweet sounds in the midst of it all.

"*Scenery is fine, but human nature is finer.*"

—John Keats

I was recently looking at some photographs that I took last summer when I was visiting a chateau, in the Loire Valley of France. On top of the chateau, there is a beautiful view, as the verdant beauty of the valley spills before the eye like an immoderate painting, colors and shapes everywhere. I took out my camera to record the moment, and upon looking at the developed film after I returned, was not more than a little annoyed and embarrassed to see that in what would have been the best shot, a couple appears in the corner, passionately locked in a kiss that appears to be a bit excessive.

The more I viewed the photograph, however, I began to see that the beauty of the valley paled in comparison to the sheer loveliness of that kiss, for it dawned on me that land and buildings can change or be destroyed, but love cannot.

12

"Her sins, which are many, are for-given; for she loved much."

—Luke 7:47

Most of us live with regret of one form or another: missed opportunities, "what-if's", sorrow surrounding pain we may have caused another. And perhaps the most terrible regret that we face is that regret which surrounds someone who is no longer with us. If only I could say I'm sorry, we think, things would be much better.

But, we should know, the love that spurs us on to want to make things right, this love has the ability to reach back through time and heal what was hurting, restore what was broken. So the key to staring down regret is to make sure that we never stray from love's gentle hope, love's amazing promise.

"*To me every hour of the light and dark is a miracle, / Every cubic inch of space a miracle.*"

—Walt Whitman

Apparently miracles just don't seem to happen as much as they used to. When Jesus was around they were a nearly everyday occurrence for Him. And after His Ascension, the members of the fledgling early Church were known to bring a few about as well. And what about the saints? They are a virtual storehouse of miraculous activity.

But those were simpler times, and people were simpler, we say. What many people thought of as miraculous back then can be achieved by other, not-so-spectacular ways today, we say.

That doesn't mean that they're not miracles, if you ask me. Sometimes in trying to explain everything away, we miss sight of just how wondrous the world can be. And just how possible it is for us to receive a miracle when we most need one.

14

"After all there is but one race—humanity."

—George Moore

I did a summer chaplaincy program at Northwestern Memorial Hospital in Chicago a few years ago. Every morning when I would walk to the hospital, I would be besieged by a particular street person, daily asking me for money. I never really knew what to do. Is money what he really needed? Although some of my feelings were conflicting, one thing was not: the man made me painfully aware of the gulf that separated people like him from people like me. His life was so alien to me that I could never even imagine what it was like to be him. We were so different.

Or so I thought. One day I found out that his name was Mark, which was my name at the time, and it dawned on me that this great chasm that I had imagined separating us was not so great at all—he could easily have been me, and I him.

"E'en though it be a cross / that raiseth me; / Still all my song would be, / Nearer, My God, to Thee / Nearer, My God, to Thee, / Nearer to Thee."
—Sarah Flower Adams

I long to be close to You, O Lord, but the trials of life are just too many at times. I long to be close to You, O Lord, but I can't seem to get beyond the pain. I long to be close to You, O Lord, but confusion clouds my judgment, my desire. I long to be close to You, O Lord, but sometimes the suffering is just too much.

If you long to be close to Me, He would say in return, then understand that I am no closer than in the trials, the pain, the confusion, the suffering. If you long to be close to Me, know that, through it all, you already are.

"Sing out, O heavens, and rejoice, O earth, break forth into song, you mountains."

—Isaiah 49:13

Recently I was stopped at a stop light and turned to look at the car that was in the lane next to me. In it was a man who was not only singing at the top of his lungs but he was playing an imaginary set of drums as well. I began laughing, wondering if he knew how ridiculous he looked, and just then he turned and looked at me. Instead of stopping his mind-concert and looking away embarrassed (what I clearly would have done in his position) he just continued to sing, continued to drum, staring right at my amazed eyes until the light turned green and we both moved on.

It seems to me we need to take comfort in the fact that there is so much joy in the world, even if at the moment it might not particularly be our joy. If we don't feel like singing, let us be thankful that the song is at least on the lips of others.

"To dry one's eyes and laugh at a fall, / And baffled, get up and begin again."

—Robert Browning

"If at first you don't succeed," it is said, "try, try again." And, although the sentiment expressed is a good way to go, I'm not sure the saying really gets to the heart of this failing and trying again business. It doesn't seem to take into consideration the metaphorical scraped knees and elbows (and even longer lasting wounds) that are part and parcel of falling. It doesn't seem to take into account that some of the ways we fail are in our relations with other people, and the confusion, sadness, joy, and ending of these relations.

But still, all in all—we must get up and begin again. To not do so is to die.

18

"By the rivers of Babylon, there we sat and wept."

—Psalm 136

Early Christian writers often talk about the "gift of tears," a notion that is perhaps difficult for many modern thinkers to embrace. We live in a society where tears are seen as weakness, surrounded by people who see some sort of courage and strength in not crying. Be strong. Get over it.

But these, our ancestors in the faith, knew that tears were a physical way of showing just how deeply we have been touched. Touched by sadness. Touched by joy. Touched by confusion. Touched by doubt. Touched by hope. Touched by gratitude. Yes, in those places deep within us where tears are born, we are so touched that merely thinking or talking about it doesn't seem quite enough. And so comes the tears, a testimony to the God who can touch us to our very core.

"*G*od is not unjust; he will not forget your work and the love you have shown him by your service, past and present, to his holy people."

—Hebrews 6:10

When I was in the parish I worked with a delightful nun named Sister Justine. Herself in her 70's, Sister Justine's main mission was to care for those she referred to as "the old," although some were no older than she. I learned a great deal about true compassion when I would accompany her on her rounds. She offered a listening ear when needed, and wasn't afraid to offer some challenging words when called for. And, when the lives of her flock were over, she offered to read the Scriptures at the funeral.

I used to wonder how she could work so tirelessly with people and then watch them slip away into death over and over again. Then it dawned on me that her caring for the living and her continual care for them after death spoke of a God whose care for us is constant and never-ending.

"He has robbed death of its power and has brought life and immortality into clear light through the gospel."

—2 Timothy 1:10

How hazy it must have appeared to so many of our ancestors, this notion of a resurrection of the dead. In the course of their daily struggles, their living of life as they had for generations, the questions of eternity had to hang over their heads like a collective fog, obscuring the light from radiating in its fullest. What would happen when they died? Would they pay for their sins, and the sins of their fathers? Was their hope that their spirit could live on?

While they knew the haze of uncertainty, we are blessed to know the clear light of the gospel promise of Jesus Christ. Death has indeed been robbed of its power, and, even though it takes a terrible toll on us, the living, we must never doubt the illuminating power of that light.

"*The poetry of earth is never dead.*"

—John Keats

Some of my happiest childhood memories revolve around time spent at my grandparents' cabin on Patterson Bay, a little bay off of the Illinois River. The days there were magical: fishing, walking, and the general running around of which children are masters. My cousin Christopher and I used to walk out into woods that were completely surrounded, for the most part, by water. If I close my eyes, I can still get a sense of it all: the smell of the water and insect repellant, the sensation of the wet mud oozing through my toes, the feeling of the muggy heat running down my back in rivulets of sweat. And when there are times when I have a keen awareness of how transitory so many things in life can be, it soothes me to know that the bay and the woods and the heat are still there, even though my grandparents no longer are.

21

A
U
G
U
S
T

"Jesus, if this is how you treat your friends, it's no wonder you have so few."

—Teresa of Avila

"Take up your cross and follow me, mine is the way to life." So goes one of the refrains we sing periodically in church. And we have sung it over and over again, and I'm sure most of us don't give too much thought to the words, even as we sing them. We can sing of the Cross. We can preach eloquently about how it is the necessary instrument of our salvation. We can agree that without the ugliness of the Cross there could have been no beautiful Resurrection morn.

But in the depths of our hearts, it's still pretty hard to take, this Cross business. Couldn't there be a better way to draw closer to Jesus than this?

Perhaps we think there could be a better way. But God obviously does not. In setting the Cross in our midst, He shows us the true meaning of a friendship that never dies.

"Who rises from prayer a better man, his prayer is answered."

—George Meredith

Help me heal, I cried to God, and yet my heart still felt broken, my prayer apparently unanswered. Help me understand it all, I cried to God, and yet still was filled with confusion, my prayer apparently unanswered. Help me to accept it all, I cried to God, and yet still I seethed in anger, my prayer apparently unanswered.

And through it all I noticed something happening: I began to heal a bit, but not all; I began to understand a bit; but not all; I began to accept a bit, but not all. My prayers were apparently answered, but not all. Not yet.

24

"He comforts us in our afflictions and thus enables us to comfort those who are in trouble, with the same consolations we have received from him."

—2 Corinthians 1:4

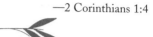

It never seems to get any easier, know-ing what to say to people who have suffered loss in their lives. All too often we stand in a receiving line at a funeral home and are never entirely certain what we will say when we get to the grieving family. And when we speak our words seem sterile, meaningless, and seem to offer scant solace.

But even if we feel our words leave something to be desired, our presence does not. Our presence to people who grieve is a reflection of the presence of a God who will not leave His children alone, but desires to be with them.

It's all connected, God's care for us, and our care for one another. Let us never forget this, because this—not nec-essarily the words that we or others say—is what really matters.

"How lovely is your dwelling place, O Lord, God of hosts."

—Psalm 83

I have been in grand, ancient cathedrals, their spires rising to a heaven that can seem quite remote, but inspiring nonetheless. I have been in small country chapels, their cramped spaces suggesting a God who is so very close to us. And in all of them—from soaring gothic heights to understated simplicity, from gold gilt to time-worn wood—there is something calming, powerful, promising. That God is present in a sunset, or a lake, or the laugh of a child is true; but God's presence in houses of prayer all over the world is unique, distinctive. Let us never lose sight of the fact that God's dwelling place is lovely, and can offer us a solace and hope that we can find nowhere else.

"Jesus called the disciples over to him and said: 'My heart is moved with pity for the crowd.'"

—Mark 8:1-2

Maybe they were hungry, their empty stomachs growling out in need. Maybe they were searching, their empty souls longing to be filled. Maybe they were sorrowing, their empty hearts longing to beat with love once again. Whatever their needs, He sensed them, and He felt pity. And He filled that within them that needed to be filled. And they walked away from the encounter much the better for it.

We, too, face emptiness. And the same pity that Jesus extended to those people so long ago is extended to us as well. If we let Him fill our needs, we too will find that we will walk away from the encounter much the better for it. Our challenge, of course, is that we have to come to Him in the first place.

"All of us fall short in many respects."
—James 3:2

I remember my mother told me once to do something insignificant—take my shoes off before coming into the house or pick up some toys—and I ignored her. After she died I began to feel a disproportionate amount of guilt over this one incident. Why couldn't I have done what she asked, I asked myself? If only I could turn back the clock.

Most of us have a hard time forgiving our own mistakes, but our mistakes can take on an epic proportion when they surround someone who is no longer physically around to apologize to. But we do all indeed fall short in many respects, and the things that plague us in regards to loved ones who have gone before us aren't necessarily as terrible as we think. We constantly need to steel ourselves in the practice of putting things into perspective.

28 *"I wept and I believed."*

—François René de Chateaubriand

Chateaubriand used these words to describe his conversion to Christianity, and they touch upon a rather ancient tradition, that being the connection between faith and tears. We live in a world where tears can be misunderstood, even considered bad form. But if we profess our faith with our whole heart and soul and body, then the body's expression of grand truths and realities just might take the form of tears. Tears of joy at the wonders of being a child of the light. Tears of gratitude at being uniquely God's own. Tears of sadness at letting go of someone we love. Tears of anguish over pain suffered. And so we can say that we wept *because* we believed.

> *"Most people want security in this world, not liberty."*
>
> —H.L. Mencken

Throughout much of grade school through high school, my father and stepmother left for work before I got out of bed in the morning. As they were preparing to leave for the day, they would yell upstairs to make sure that I was awake, and take off. I didn't feel as alone, however, as this may make it sound, because every morning when I came downstairs, there was always lunch money and a note waiting for me. The note could say anything from, "Have a good day!" to "Don't forget to unload the dishwasher," but whatever its content, it always had the same effect on me, that of making me feel protected, loved somehow.

Even when God seems far away, the world is filled with signs that we are protected and loved. We must make sure we don't run out the door without paying attention to them.

"Sing away sorrow, cast away care."
—Miguel de Cervantes

Brother Matthew admittedly doesn't have the best singing voice in the world. But when Brother Matthew opens his mouth to sing, you can see all over his face that he really *believes* what it is he's singing. In the midst of drudgery and routine and work and perhaps even a little sorrow now and then, he nevertheless has the faith to open his mouth and sing, "For his love endures for ever!" and I know it's true. Even if I have a hard time seeing (or hearing) that love in my own song, it is a comfort and strength for me to see it and hear it in his. And what a wonderful melody that makes it, because it is ultimately an echo of the song God sings to woo the world.

"The strongest and sweetest songs yet remain to be sung."

—Walt Whitman

I remember the day my mother died, climbing my favorite tree, the one in between our yard and the yard of our neighbor, Miss Crain. As I perched myself in the midst of the tree's leafy familiarity, I felt as if life would never again be good. How could I ever enjoy a game again, smile? How could I ever really know what it means to love, since the one I loved most was gone? It was a sad day: a seven-year old had decided that his life was over.

It wasn't over, of course. And I don't know if it would have made a difference that day, if I could see into the futures and know of all the games, all the smiles, all the love that would come my way. It probably wouldn't have made a difference then, but it does now.

SEPTEMBER

"God keeps his word."

—2 Corinthians 1:18

God said, "Let there be light," and there was. God said, "It is not good to be alone, I will make you a partner," and a partner was created. God said, "I will bring the Israelites to a land flowing with milk and honey," and the Israelites settled in just such a place. God said, "I will send them my Son," and Jesus came into the world. Jesus said, "Your sins are forgiven," and they were, they are. Jesus said, "I am the way," and it's true.

If God, through Jesus, kept all of these words (and countless others as well) then we can be certain that when He said, "Anyone who believes in me shall never die," He meant it.

"I am the vine, you are the branches."

—John 15:5

I had never really been in a vineyard before, but not long after arriving at the monastery was sent to ours to pick grapes for the harvest. On one hand it was an awful experience (sweltering heat, dripping humidity, angry bees and wasps swarming the outer grapes that had burst open). On the other hand, however, it was fascinating, because I could see close up just how reliant upon the vine the branches were.

Another thing I noticed, however, was that the best grapes were the ones that were buried deep within the mass of branches, with the other branches surrounding it acting as a shield against the severity of the elements. And it dawned on me that it was not only the vine that helps the branches bear fruit, but the branches themselves. Not a bad lesson for us branches.

"For you has he commanded his angels, to keep you in all your ways."
—Psalm 90

Angels have become big business. What many once considered a quaint little religious belief has exploded into the pop-culture's consciousness. We have movies and television shows about angels. We have posters and t-shirts and wrist watches with angels on them. We have books encouraging people to get in touch with the angel inside of them. To be honest, I'm not sure what any of this has to do with the real angels that attend to God. I'm not sure any of it speaks to the deep theological significance of these created, incorporeal beings, and their mission, their message, to us.

But it does speak of our need to know that God is watching out for us. It is a comfort to know that—whatever angels do or do not look like—somehow God's care for us extends in ways that we can't know or understand, but is most certainly real.

4

> "*There is a wisdom of the head, and ... a wisdom of the heart.*"
>
> —Charles Dickens

A few days after my mother died, I remember some adult saying to me that the past few days had been very hard and tiring for my father, and I needed to be especially good so that he didn't have to deal with any more than he was already dealing with. Even as a seven year old, this made sense to me, seemed to possess a wisdom and common sense that even I could grasp. They went on to say, however, that I shouldn't be crying as much as I was, I should try extra hard not to. Whereas the wisdom of doing all I could to help my father seemed to make sense to me, this seemed a bit harsh; after all I didn't *want* to cry. I ran off and ran into my Gramps, who took one look at me and knew exactly what I needed. "Let it out, Spark Plug," he said to me. And I did. And with my tears came a recognition of true wisdom.

"Pain is short, and joy is eternal."
—Johann Christoph Friedrich von Schiller

With these words von Schiller ended *The Maid of Orleans*, his play about Joan of Arc. And though the story of this heroic girl is inspiring, it is a bit difficult for us to connect with her way of thinking. She heard voices; she was always courageous; she was a saint. Those of us who toil without voices and courage and sainthood might find it difficult to see just how fleeting pain is, especially when we are in the middle of it. Leave that thinking to the saints—I don't want to suffer any more.

However, the exceptional sanctity of Saint Joan doesn't take away the truth of either the transitory nature of suffering, or the eternal nature of joy. Perhaps if we wish to make such a connection, we should work harder at being saints ourselves.

6

"When he expelled the man, he settled him east of the garden of Eden."

—Genesis 3:24

I remember thinking my senior year in college that life could not possibly be better than it was then. I had very little responsibility, I was surrounded by my friends, my family was doing fine. And it was glorious, this constant happiness, this little piece of paradise that I had staked out.

Then it started happening. My grandmother died. My sister got sick. And all of a sudden paradise was no longer my address, but a place I used to live. As time continued I found myself longing for those days: Remember our senior year in college?

I realize now that the paradise I perceived was real, but not lasting. How much easier life has been since I have accepted that I will never live there again until the end of my life (and then a much greater paradise), but rather accept the reality of settling just east of there.

"In looking on the happy autumn fields / And thinking of the days that are no more."

—Alfred, Lord Tennyson

My favorite time of the year for walking is the early autumn, when it is easy to get lost in the sights and smells of an Indian summer day. The cool wind blows across my face the aroma of burning leaves, and if I close my eyes, the smell almost seems to have a life of its own; it is no longer just a smell, but has acquired sights and sounds, colors and memories as well. The leaves under my feet are as musical instruments, and I am transfixed by their song. Everything around me attests to one thing: summer is truly over. This could be happy (a testimony to the wondrous cycle of life) or sad (a testimony to the inevitability of death). Being able to realize it is both is grace.

8

"Jacob was left there alone. Then some man wrestled with him until the break of dawn."

—Genesis 32:24

What did Jacob think he was doing, wrestling with God? How foolish to enter into such a struggle, wrought, as it was, with certain strife, incalculable struggle. And yet, so passionate was Jacob's desire to know God, to receive His blessing, that he didn't seem to care what it might look like, how foolish or futile it might appear. Even if Jacob knew that he couldn't win, and would most likely end up limping away from the encounter (which he did), he knew that the fight was worth it, that in the struggle could be found grace.

God's will is not always easy to understand, and it is no disrespect to question what's going on in our lives. Like Jacob, we need to have the passion to stick with the fight, to face the hard answers that come about as we wrestle with what God wants from us. That limping grace can be ours as well.

"But Moses said to God, 'Who am I that I should go to Pharaoh and lead the Israelites out of Egypt?'"

—Exodus 3:11

His mental checklist—the one that had the reasons that he should not go into Egypt—had to have been significant: I am not well loved in Egypt; It's too far away; My sheep will suffer; I have no great army to help me; I don't possess the necessary eloquence. And to counteract this list, God had a list of his own: I will be with you. I will be with you. I will be with you. Moses was powerless against such a list.

Like Moses, we all too often wonder how it is we can do the things we're supposed to. Some days, just getting out of bed in the morning can be a nearly overwhelming task. And we might have a long list of reasons why we just can't go on.

And God's list remains: I am with you. I am with you. I am with you. And we are powerless against such a list. And in this powerlessness we find strength.

"There's a good time coming, boys! A good time coming."

—Charles Mackay

At my mother's visitation, I remember a woman from my church enveloping me in a large hug, smashing my face against her lilac-scented bosom, saying, "You've got your whole life ahead of you, you're going to have a wonderful life!" I didn't particularly want to hear that at the time (and I had been hearing far too much of it as it was). In the midst of a natural sadness, the last thing I wanted to reflect on was the fact that my life was going to be wonderful again.

Even if it was true, which it was. Although that day a life filled with joy was quite beyond my grasp, it clearly was a reality. The sadness would pass, and life would continue. I know now how true that is, and, perhaps, I knew it that day as well, even if I didn't want to hear it.

"*We are afflicted in every way possible, but we are not crushed; full of doubts, we never despair.*"

—2 Corinthians 4:8

If only there were a better way. If only we could expect to live a life free from affliction, free from doubt. If only there were some other model of how to live, one that didn't include some of the less attractive elements like suffering and death. What would such a model look like, I wonder?

It certainly wouldn't look the model of Christ, who is the only model for a Christian. That Christ was afflicted and yet not crushed, and that Christ doubted and yet never despaired doesn't make our afflictions and doubts any easier. But it does make their outcome more certain, if we believe.

"God gave a Loaf to every Bird /—
But just a Crumb—to me —"
—Emily Dickinson

I used to look at my friend Godfrey's life with an admiration that bordered on envy. He came from a wonderful family, and divorce and death hadn't seemed to have touched it too much. There didn't seem to be a lot of the internal bickering and intrigue among his siblings that constantly seemed to rear its ugly head in my family. He was so fortunate, I thought, and often seemed to get the whole loaf, fresh and warm from the oven, bountiful in its quantity.

I know now that all of the things that have happened to me, although not always pleasant, nevertheless helped make me who I am and—hopefully—better. When I find I long for the whole loaf, it serves me well to remember that the crumbs can be pretty satisfying at times.

"The reign of God is like a mustard seed which someone took and sowed in his field."

—Matthew 13:31

The reality of this parable is quite evident. Two thousand years ago, a man with a simple message of love asked people to look at their world, their God, a little differently. And from that humble beginning in an isolated part of the world two thousand years ago came the Church, which has spread that original message over all the earth.

This amazing growth isn't chance; it's a pattern. And this pattern is played out over and over again, every time we make small attempts in our life, confident that somehow God can and will smile on our efforts, and bring to birth possibilities in us that we ourselves cannot even fully imagine.

14

"*Why stay we on the earth except to grow?*"

—Robert Browning

We are born on this earth knowing nothing, completely dependent. We grow into childhood, and we begin to see how the things that we are learning (tying our shoes, looking both ways before crossing the street) can apparently pay off, and so we are dependent upon others to learn more still. We grow into adolescence, and, suddenly, we find that we know more than anyone else, and much of what we are supposed to learn (algebra, Shakespeare) is an apparent waste of time. We grow into adulthood, and we realize that there is much to learn if we want to get ahead in the world. And we grow into our old age, once again dependent on others, mindful of all that we have learned, mindful of all that we don't know, mindful that life itself—good and bad—has been a most wondrous teacher, even when we found the lessons harsh.

"A man with God is always in the majority."

—John Knox

"I've never lived by myself before," a widow once said to me. At home, she had been the oldest of eight children; eventually, she mothered nine herself. And now, her husband was gone, her children were grown, and she was alone. That her children lived not too far away offered scant solace at that point; she would be rattling around her big old house alone.

I didn't quite know what to say to her, and she was clearly expecting me to say something. And so, I told her what I know to be true: We are never alone, for God is with us. I, personally, can't always see or hear Him, and sometimes I wonder if He is really there or not somewhere else, but I have to believe that He is here, or some days would be pretty difficult to get through.

*"My brothers, count it pure joy when
you are involved in every sort of trial."*
—James 1:2

It seems a little optimistic to me, counting it as joy when involved in trials. I can understand seeing how trials mold and shape us. I can see how undergoing trials makes us stronger. I can even see that life's sweetness can seem all the sweeter when it is interspersed in between trials. But joy? That seems a little far-fetched.

But, a brief glance at the dictionary links joy with a feeling of well-being. Maybe that is not so far-fetched after all, not if we grasp that even in the midst of trials God is with us, teaching us, sustaining us, and—in some mysterious way often beyond my understanding—loving us. Our beings can definitely feel well about that.

"*Man was made for joy and woe, /
And when this we rightly know /
Through the world we safely go.*"
—William Blake

Expectations can often get the best of us, often be the source of inordinate amounts of disappointment. As children we expect to get everything we ask for at Christmastime, and can frequently be disappointed in the midst of wonderful gifts. As adults we expect that people should be this way or that, and be disappointed in the midst of some wonderful gifts.

When we expect life to be perfect and painless, we can be extremely disappointed. If we pray for the grace to change our expectations, it is surprising what gifts we might just discover. God does not disappoint.

"One day Jesus was praying in a certain place."

—Matthew 11:1

For some it's the quiet coolness of an empty church, creaking pews singing some insight. For some it's the expansive verdancy of a lush field, chirping crickets singing some possibility. For some it's a park in a busy city, blaring horns singing some certainty. For some it's a child's room, sleeping breath singing some love. For some it's the sober serenity of a cemetery, voices of the past singing some loss. Wherever it is, most of us have that "certain" place—the place where we can be ourselves, the place where we can question life's events, the place where we can remember people, the place where we can express joys and sorrows. And, ultimately, in being ourselves, in questioning life, in remembering people, in expressing joys and sorrows, we find that our certain place is made special by the God who is most certainly present for all of it—and all of us.

"*Indeed, like clay in the hand of the potter, so are you in my hand, house of Israel.*"

—Jeremiah 18:6

I wonder if the people of the prophet Jeremiah's day found this image of the potter and the clay at all comforting. If they gave much thought to the process by which the clay becomes something, they may have preferred a different approach altogether, say, a nice painting or something. Because clay is knocked around, torn off, put back together, and shaped with no apparent regard for the material itself. If too much is there, part of it is torn off and thrown away, and more can be added to areas where more is called for. And then, after all the pushing and pulling, and tearing and shaping, it is thrown in the fire. What could possibly be comforting about this?

Nothing, except, of course, that at the end of it all you have a piece of such beauty that the former clay looks downright plain in comparison.

> *"The Lord is my shepherd, there is nothing I shall want."*
>
> —Psalm 22

What a beautiful, familiar piece of scripture is the Good Shepherd psalm. What a comfort it has been to countless individuals, who take solace in the image of a compassionate Savior, gently laying a straying sheep around his neck, bringing him back to the safety, the warmth, the sheer love of the flock. The gentleness of the shepherd is captivating indeed.

But what about those times in our lives which "gentle" doesn't exactly describe? What about those times when genuine struggle and hardship make us long for the answers that don't seem to be on the lips of a soft shepherd? What about when we don't need to be tenderly caressed so much as sternly challenged? The psalm still speaks to us. It's just that at these times the shepherd isn't carrying us, He's pushing and prodding us with His staff.

"And the Lord said to Moses, 'Take the staff and assemble the community… and in their presence order the rock to yield waters.'"

—Numbers 20:8

It stood there, this rock, large, unyielding, hard, dead. And it stood as a testament to a community that itself had grown unyielding and hard. And as if to say to them, "I can bring forth life from even the hardest of hearts," he had that rock struck with a staff, and from what appeared to be dead came life, spilling out, joining with the rivers of their souls, refreshing them.

When we think that life has hardened our hearts, that no one can penetrate them, we are fooling ourselves. Because the same God who brought forth water from a rock and brought forth life from a man's execution, can tap into even the hardest of hearts, bringing forth amazing possibilities for us to drink in.

"*The supreme happiness of life is the conviction that we are loved.*"

—Victor Hugo

I have memories of my mother reading to me, with me, sharing the wonders of writing with someone for the first time. I have memories of my grandma baking for me, my tongue enraptured with the sweetness of cinnamon and spice. I have memories of my grandpa telling me stories, giving me a notion of what it meant to be a part of his family, a part of him.

But those are memories. I also have recent experience of my father teasing me, making me laugh at my own follies. I have recent experience of my step-mother bringing cookies and underwear to the monastery, taking care of me. The one thing that ties all of this together is love. And I know that the love of my current experience is the same as the love of my memories, and that it goes on. And this makes me aware of that which is clearly stronger than death.

"You must endure a little of my folly. Put up with me, I beg you!"
—2 Corinthians 11:1

Patience is a virtue for everyone, not just for us. And so it is that there are times when we are going to be moody, temperamental, overly emotional, disagreeable, and just downright hard to be around. And all of these things can be multiplied ten-fold when they come on the heels of (or particularly because of) loss in our lives. But just as we are patient with the shortcomings of those we love, we need to understand that they will be patient with us. And if there are times when we are not the best people we could be, so be it. We'll get better, with a little patience.

24

"The whole of history is incomprehensible without him [Jesus]."

—Ernest Renan

When I was in grade school, one always counted ancient years in terms of "B.C."—before Christ. This accounting seemed to be fine with me and most everyone I knew, but by the time I got to college, "B.C." had become "B.C.E."—before the common era, and something seemed to be missing in my mind. It seemed to me that by adding that "E" we are taking away the context of most of the history of the last 2000 years.

If we do subscribe that history is incomprehensible without Him, how much more are our very lives incomprehensible without Him as well. We cannot make sense of the things that happen to us in this world without Him, who is the very context of the world, and time, and history itself.

"Soldiers of Christ, arise, / And put your armor on."

—Charles Wesley

In days gone by, there seemed to be a lot more battle imagery when dealing with matters of the faith. The early monastics went into the desert to battle demons. Those confirmed during a particular time in history were encouraged to become Soldiers of Christ, fighting the battle of faith. In recent years, however, much of this battle talk has gone out of fashion, probably due to the paradox of the Prince of Peace encouraging a fight.

But a fight it can be, this battle with forces in the world that would promote darkness over light, despair over hope. And so maybe it is not such a bad thing to ready ourselves for the battle, armed not with weapons of destruction, but with righteousness, faith, and hope—armaments worthy of our King.

"Although the world is full of suffering, it is full also of the overcoming of it."

—Helen Keller

Her world was not, as it is for so many young people, a bright portrait of stunning possibilities; it was a cruel montage of black on black. She heard not the enticing music of reckless joy, but only the mocking of silence. She spoke, not in the trilling arrogance of freedom, but in the labored breath of bondage. And yet, in spite of it all, Helen Keller was able to rise above her suffering, and offer hope to so many people.

The courage and strength of conviction that enabled her to achieve so much rests in each of us. To tap into it, we need only use our eyes to see what is of ultimate importance, our ears to hear the true message, our lips to speak of the confusing brilliance of a love that never dies.

"I live and love in God's peculiar light."

—Michelangelo

The lines are memorized. The costume adjusted. And then, with a rush of adrenaline, the actor steps onto the stage and, in the harshness of the lights, makes us believe he is someone he is not: Hamlet, Othello, Stanley Kowalski. And as long as they are all there, these masks that conceal who he really is, we believe he is someone else, and even the light that can expose so much keeps his secret.

God's light is different. Because unlike the light of the stage that compliments the masks, God's light, God's love, penetrates our deepest selves, and our masks do nothing to conceal who we are from Him, or who He is from us. It is in the authenticity that the light calls forth in us that we bring everything we are—joys, sorrows, energy, sloth, faith, doubt—and hold it up to be illumined.

"The night is dark, and I am far from home; / Lead thou me on!"
—John Henry Cardinal Newman

Just a few hours after my mother died, my father took my brother and me for a milkshake at Deck's Drug Store, as he had done so many times before. As I walked into Deck's, I felt as if I had never been there before. The familiarity of this treasured place had disappeared. News of the death had reached the drugstore before we had, and my Dad, brother and I were met by the eyes of patrons red from crying. Why were they crying, I wondered, it was my mother, not theirs, and Dad told us that we had to be brave, and so I couldn't cry.

But later, back home, I ran to my climbing tree, and there, above it all, I was able to cry out in sheer anger at a world that would leave small boys motherless. And I could do this because I was home, where I could be myself.

"I love everything that's old: old friends, old times, old manners, old books, old wines."

—Oliver Goldsmith

There are those who would say that dwelling on the past is a useless waste of our time, that the things and the people who have gone before us will never again return, and so we should forget them. I would agree that dwelling in the past—that making those people and events from the past our measuring stick for absolutely everything in the present—is not the healthiest of attitudes.

But there can be no denying that within the old times lie important keys to our current times, and to our future. If we are to understand ourselves, we clearly need to understand where we've been. If we are to understand the influence others have had on us, we clearly need to understand where that influence began. If we are to understand how to live without some of the people and things we once held so dear, we need to understand what it meant to live with them.

30

"'T want me, 'twas the Lord. I always told him, 'I trust to you. I don't know where to go or what to do, but I expect you to lead me,' and he always did."

—Harriet Tubman

After my ordination, I had planned out the next 50 years of my life with great precision. I knew exactly where I wanted to be, what I wanted to be doing, and exactly how to get there. God had a place in it all, of course, but I discerned His will for me to be just a reflection of what I wanted for myself.

Two years after I was ordained I was diagnosed with cancer, and all my plans were cast into the murky light of confusion. Maybe things were not as settled as I had naively imagined. Maybe God's will was really God's and not my own. I had no choice but to follow His lead, as painful as it was.

All kinds of things can happen that turn our lives upside down. The only sure way to righting them again is to expect God to lead us out of it all. He always will.

OCTOBER

"Love kindled by virtue always kindles another, provided that its flame appear outwardly."

—Dante Alighieri

Maybe it's the soft touch of a mother, melting away fear with the strength of an embrace. Maybe it's the encouraging words of a father, making the harshness of the world not seem so debilitating. Maybe it's the passionate clasp of a lover, whose arms bring about the certainty of acceptance. Whatever the case, most of us have been blessed at one time or another with manifestations of love. And what a difference they can make in our lives, what comfort and surety they can provide, especially in times of suffering and doubt.

And—the cycle goes—when we have been touched in some way by love, we need to touch others. To do so keeps love alive in a world all too often hostile to its presence. To not do so is nothing short of ingratitude.

"Do not ask me to abandon or forsake you! For wherever you go, I will go, wherever you lodge, I will lodge, your people shall be my people, and your God my God."

—Ruth 1:16

How much easier it would have been for her, this Ruth, if she had just gone back home. Widowed, among a strange people with a strange God, with no land to call her own, and no prospect of finding a husband through the regular channels, it would have been so much easier for her to return to what had once been her home, easier to find a life for herself there, to begin again. But Ruth clung to her mother-in-law, uttering powerful words of fidelity, thus clinging to her God and His strange ways.

There are times when it would be easier for us to go back to our old ways, to turn our back on this strange God. But, like Ruth, we need to realize that the real freedom, the real growth, comes, not in freeing ourselves from Him, but in clinging to Him.

"When other helpers fail, and comforts flee, / Help of the helpless, O abide with me."

—Henry Francis Lyte

I first met Alice when she was nearing the day of her death, from lung cancer. Thrice married and thrice divorced, with no children, she was crusty, angry, and utterly alone. At first she didn't want to talk with me; I represented an organized religion that she wanted no part of. More and more I managed to hear her story, though, and I was saddened by how lonely she made life sound. I made a resolution that she would not die alone, that I would be there.

Alice died while I was at a nearby restaurant, having dinner with friends. The next day, hearing of the loss I was angered and distraught—I didn't want her to be alone—and I told the floor nurse how upset I was that no one had called me.

"She didn't die alone," the nurse told me, "Jesus was with her." I believed her.

4

*"Save that from yonder ivy-mantled
tow'r / The moping owl does to the
moon complain."*

—Thomas Gray

It is, in many circles, an unpardonable
offense to complain about anything,
with the possible exceptions of the government and the Church. Everyone has
their own problems, some would say, so
I am not particularly interested in hearing yours.

But disappointment, regret, and pain
are a part of the human existence. And if
we do not express our disappointment,
regret, and pain to others it can—in the
unchecked recesses of our hearts and
minds—build up so that it becomes distorted. Better to risk mildly annoying
others with our complaints than allow
these complaints to control us.

"A good book is the best of friends, the same today and forever."
—Martin Farquhar Tupper

Every year, right after Easter, I read *The Wind in the Willows*, the children's book by Kenneth Grahame. My annual reading of it marks the passage of time for me, and I bring with each reading another year of experiences, of good times and bad times, that makes me view the story and its delightful characters in new and different ways. My life may change drastically from year to year, but I know that Mr. Mole and Mr. Rat will remain constant, though I may view them with eyes changed by time.

In a world where far too much is transitory, we all need to find something that we know will always be there. A book is as good a place as any to start.

"Ad astra per aspera." [To the stars through hardships.]

—Latin Proverb

Sir Edmund Hilary's reported answer as to why he climbed Mount Everest ("Because it's there") seems, at first glance, a bit lacking in substance. He spent years in preparation and great amounts of money. He endured great physical struggles, indeed, even risked death to climb that mountain. And all of it because it was there? Many things in life are there, it doesn't necessarily mean we are going to tackle them, though.

But, even if the literal logic of the statement is lacking, the metaphorical power of climbing the mountain suffuses it with great symbolism. Because, like that mountain—just there—so, too are the small and not-so-small challenges we face every day. And we scale them because they are there, because not to would be to allow life to defeat us, because walking around the mountain is not always an option.

"Choose life, then, that you and your descendants may live, by loving the Lord, your God, heeding his voice, and holding fast to him."

—Deuteronomy 30:19-20

Life's choices used to be so much simpler when I was younger: What TV show am I going to watch after school? Will I go for a bike ride, or swimming today? What shirt am I going to wear? As I grew older the questions became more demanding: Where am I going to college? What am I going to major in? What am I going to do with my life? What role does God play in any of this?

But in it all—from the simplest questions to the deep, existential pondering of life and vocation—the choices, though not always simple, are nonetheless clear. We can choose to give into God's life, loving and holding fast to Him, even when we don't understand Him, or we can choose to have no part of Him, the ramifications of which are death. It is in living out this basic choice that all of life's questions get answered.

7

O
C
T
O
B
E
R

"The music in my heart I bore / Long after it was heard no more."

—William Wordsworth

I remember distinctly the night before I began first grade, my mother singing to me before I went to bed. The song was of a familiar tune, but she had changed the words to fit the solemn occasion of my beginning school. I remember her voice as being lovely, soothing, quite melodious. I have been asked often where I got my singing voice from, and based on this experience I always replied that I got it from my mother.

My sister recently told me that our mother's voice was not quite as sweet as I remembered it. At first I was devastated, but the more I thought about it it didn't seem to matter all that much. That her song is in me is undeniable, and this makes it sweet nonetheless.

> *"If a tree dies, plant another in its place."*
>
> —Carl von Linné

It's easy to speak about trees, and naïve to think that this analogy can be extended to people. Or is it? It is true that when we have to say goodbye to a loved one, we must take leave of so much: companionship, security, connectedness, support. But what about love, memories, laughter, inspiration? What about recognizing those traits within that person that so affected us that we are forever changed, and will carry those things with us until we too join them in death's finality?

In recognizing that about a person which lives on after him—in celebrating it—we are planting the seed of healing in our lives, making sure that love continues and grows anew.

10

"'Tis always morning somewhere in the world."

—Richard Henry Hengist Horne

I hated going to bed as a child—still do—especially in the summer months. Summer days were filled with such wonder and action that the setting of the sun signaled an unfortunate end. Playing our games we would keep one eye on the game and one expectantly on the western skyline, praying for the sun to cease its downward trek, dreading that moment when mothers and fathers and older sisters began yelling out the names of the neighborhood children and washing up would commence.

It was a comfort to me in those days to look to where the sun was setting and imagine that over there, beyond it, a summer's day was just beginning for some lucky kid. Although the odious tasks of washing and teeth brushing awaited me, I liked knowing that it was a new day filled with light for others.

It was in Jerusalem that it would all happen: the condemnation, the mocking, the flogging, the pain, the death. Jerusalem, that seductive city that had seen the death of so many prophets, was to witness the death of another. But instead of shying away from it all, instead of bypassing this city with all the terror it would soon hold, Jesus told the Twelve what the ultimate price for following Him was: they, too, were to go to Jerusalem, to face it all. It was a heavy price to pay.

It still is a heavy price today for all of us who, trying to face the struggles of our own Jerusalem, often feel burdened by the weight of the journey. Our only hope, our only consolation, is the same hope and consolation of the Twelve, and the hope and consolation of so many people before us: we do not make the journey alone.

12

"The whole secret of the study of nature lies in learning how to use one's eyes."

—George Sand

One of the rites of passage at St. Anthony High School is the sophomore year bug collection. In the months before the collection is due, it is not unusual to see mothers clandestinely trading margarine containers and baggies in the grocery store, as if trafficking in some contraband substance. "I'll give you this Japanese beetle. Do you know anyone who has a horse fly?" Once a year students and their parents become experts at seeing minute differences between the different varieties of bugs, a mark here, a wing shape there.

It seems to me that human nature—especially our own—requires just such scrutiny. And so, if we find ourselves struggling where others have seemingly glided, we need to realize that perhaps we're just a slightly different variety of bug.

"Jesus said to his disciples: 'You are the salt of the earth.'"

—Matthew 5:13

"He's the salt of the earth," I've heard many times in my life, and I always smile and nod as if I know exactly what it means. But besides the obvious connection that people who are the salt of the earth are good people, I'm a little unclear of what it is being salt signifies. I suppose that if salt makes bland food better, then those who are the salt of the earth somehow make the world in which we live better. It goes to follow, then, that if we need to season the sorrow that life all too often puts on our plate, then we should probably seek these people out to help us.

*"What example can I show you for
your comfort, virgin daughter Zion?
For great as the sea is your downfall;
who can heal you?"*

—Lamentations 2:13

Their wailing was great: images of
eyes worn out from weeping, of
people sitting in dust, of infants not having enough food, of tears flowing like a
river, day and night, of death and
destruction. And in the midst of this
unparalleled imagery of suffering a question arises: who can heal you? Even in
the midst of the anguished cries, the
question is cried out as well. And cried
out, I think, in a way that shows that
they know the answer already.

We all have our share of lamentations—great and small alike. In the
midst of them, let us never fear to cry
out that same question: who can heal us?
And let us pray for the grace to have
already known the answer.

"The sky is the daily bread of the eyes."
—Ralph Waldo Emerson

Just off of the monastery courtyard is a place called the Belvidere, a high arched area where one can sit and look at the valley below without being exposed to the harsher side of the elements. It is ideal for storm watching, to sit, sipping a cup of coffee and watch the sky change from gray to indigo, with large, fast-moving clouds forming patches on its darkened fabric. And, after storm has passed, what delight there is in seeing the first streaks of color peek through the clouds, the rays of the sun piercing it like shards to shattered light.

It's all there—the good and the bad—in the beauty of the sky. And how often do we walk under its majesty, and not once look upward, reveling in such a gift?

"The stone which the builders rejected has become the cornerstone."

—Psalm 117

The US Hockey Team scoring the winning goal against the favored Russians. The small-town basketball team winning the state tournament. The cyclist overcoming cancer to win the Tour de France. The world of sports is filled with such stories, stories of underdogs, of people who conventional wisdom said shouldn't have won, but won nonetheless.

And who doesn't love such a story? It touches that within us that makes us believe, if only for an instant, that absolutely anything is possible when the human spirit is pushed to excel; that even the unlikeliest of people can achieve what had once been thought to be impossible. It goes to follow, of course (even though we don't always see it) that if others can do it, we can as well, even when the task seems impossible.

"Life is made up of marble and mud."
—Nathaniel Hawthorne

I have pictures in my office of vacations and parties that I have attended over the years, beaming faces staring back at me with looks of sheer, unadulterated fun. Periodically, I find myself looking at these pictures; trying to remember what it was like to be that carefree, that relaxed, that happy; wondering why life can't be more like that, and less like what it actually often is.

These thoughts come all too frequently when we are down, it seems, obscuring at times the reality that life is filled with good and bad alike, and we won't see never ending happiness until we pass from this life into the next. Maybe, alongside photographs of smiling happy faces, we should include a few pictures of frowns, or people we don't care too much for, just to make sure we keep a balanced view of both the marble and the mud.

18

*"It's hardly in a body's pow'r. / To keep,
at times, frae being sour."*

—Robert Burns

I drove over to Ed's house as soon as I
heard of the death of his wife. A couple of his children had already arrived,
and were hovering about him, tending to
his needs in that lop-sided way that
adult children can do with their parents.
I went into the living room, walked up
to his recliner and asked him how he was
doing. He resolutely refused to take my
hand and bellowed at me, "How the hell
do you think I'm doing, you idiot?" His
children were mortified, and began talking to him like he was an unruly child,
"Dad, you shouldn't talk to Father that
way."

I, for my part, acknowledged that it
was, indeed, a stupid question, one
which maybe even called for such an
outburst on Ed's part. We are all human
and prone to anger, and I think maybe it
was just a time for Ed to be sour. And
for me to hear about it.

"'Let the man among you who has no sin be the first to cast a stone at her.' A second time he bent down and wrote on the ground."

—John 8:7-8

There were strict laws against the act in which the woman had been caught, and those laws were to be harshly enforced; she was to die. But up against this man Jesus, the way things *had* to be done didn't seem so certain; for His ways outshone the darkness of their laws, of their minds. To their definitions that day he added a far more encompassing one: God's eternal mercy. And they walked away scratching their heads as he scratched in the dirt.

In the midst of grief, the pressure to do and say the right thing can be enormous. Grieving people by definition are to act a certain way, do certain things, not do others. But these definitions mean nothing when compared to the merciful love of a God who would tell us that, if we are mindful of His presence in our lives, then we are grieving appropriately.

"The long sobs / Of the violins / Of autumn / Pierce my heart / With monotonous languor."

—Paul Verlaine

My mother's favorite season was the autumn, and, not surprisingly, many of my memories of her center around that season, filled with dying and color. But also, not surprisingly, it is the time of the year that I seem to miss her most; that the cool air, the falling leaves, and the colors of change seem to sing to me of her all-too-short presence in my life, and her all too-long-absence. And every year, as the summer packs its cloaks of hot dark green away, and autumn replaces them with her aging vestments, I know I'll feel it all the more acutely—this loss. But I also know that my mother is powerfully present in this loss, as I realize that the colors still are beautiful, even if viewed through blurred eyes.

"Come, let us return to the Lord."
—Hosea 6:1

God's love for His people can read like a bad romance novel: He woos them, they turn away; He gets angry at them; they repent; He takes them back; they turn away again. How aggravating it can be for us to read of the constant foibles of our ancestors, they who didn't seem to get the picture of how God wanted to be an intimate part of their lives. Why did this stiff-necked people forsake God over and over and over again? Didn't they have any sense?

On one hand, no, their sense was lacking. But on the other hand, they at least had the sense to know that, even if they blamed Him for their ills, they could turn to Him at any time. How easier life would be for us if we always realized that.

"Life does not cease to be funny when people die any more than it ceases to be serious when people laugh."
—George Bernard Shaw

Lucy in the chocolate factory, feverishly shoving the chocolates in her mouth as they speed by on the conveyor belt. "Did you hear the one about the travelling salesman?" A pie in the face. Crazy Uncle Ron's antics at the family reunion. Life is filled with images and instances that can bring about a dose of that most precious medicine, laughter. To let any of them slip by without giving into them, relishing them, is to be like a child stubbornly refusing to take an offered spoon of cough syrup, allowing its sweet stickiness to temper that which hurts most in us.

"Glorious things of thee are spoken, / Zion, city of our God."

—John Newton

I had a disgruntled parishioner once complain to me that I did not preach enough about heaven. As he put it, people needed to know that all the muck we had to put up with in life was going to count for something in the end, so I needed to talk more about heaven, the New Jerusalem, our eternal reward.

Not long after this his wife died after a protracted battle with cancer. I went to his house as soon as I received the news, and, while consoling him he said, "I know she is in heaven." I wondered to myself how he knew this, if preachers like myself didn't talk enough about heaven. As if reading my thoughts, he said, "All of that goodness that was in her has to go on."

Apparently I didn't need to preach to him about heaven; he preached to me.

"Every man loves what he is good at."
—Thomas Shadwell

We pride ourselves on our accomplishments. Most of us strive to be the best we can be at what it is we do, and it is a good feeling to know that we have accomplished something, that we have done our homework and are prepared to move forward into the realm of successful achievement.

That is why when we come up against grieving a loss, it can be unsettling to say the least. No matter how much we prepare, no matter how well we say we can take care of things, loss is such an all-encompassing notion that we can never really be prepared, never really know whether our accomplishments in this area are going to bear the fruit that we hope.

There is no guarantee that we will be good at grief, and we don't like that. But if we move forward with the Lord, we can be assured that He will see to it that we will do the best we can.

"Lead, kindly Light, amid the encir-cling gloom; / Lead thou me on!"
—John Henry Cardinal Newman

A couple of years ago, the power went out in the monastery affecting even the emergency exit lights. I fumbled my way out of my room to complete darkness—I literally could not see my hand held up in front of my face. How terrifying was that darkness, and I turned to go back to the familiarity of my room when I realized that I had walked too far, and could not distinguish one door from another. Way off in the distance, though, I saw a small point of light, perhaps the pen light of a fellow stumbler like myself. Whatever the case, it dawned on me that, even in extreme darkness, the smallest light could act as a veritable beacon of hope. And so I walked toward it, and somehow felt better, even though I didn't know for sure what I would find when I reached it.

"But I chose you out of the world."

—John 15:19

So often we hear the word "vocation" used in connection with ministry ("He has a vocation to be a priest") or with a career ("She has a vocation to be a teacher.") The concept of vocation goes far beyond this, however. From the Latin "to call," vocation describes that answer in all of us to do what it is we are supposed to do, to—to borrow from the Army—be all that we can be. And at the root of every Christian call is the One who calls us. The Lord may not call us to do enormous, public things, but He calls all of us to do *something*. He knows how unique we all are, and He specifically chooses us to do particular things, to bear certain crosses. When we feel it may just be too much for us, we need only remember that we were chosen for our lives, and obviously we can handle that to which we have been called.

"Once, on the sabbath, we went outside the city gate to the bank of a river, where we thought there would be a place of prayer."

—Acts of the Apostles 16:13

Some of us prefer to pray in churches, where the quiet of stone and wood can help us listen better. Some of us prefer to pray driving down the road, where the hum of motor and road are as a psalm of the continuity of God. Some of us prefer to pray lying in our bed at night, where we can imagine ourselves falling asleep in God's loving arms.

Prayer—that communication between us and God—cannot be limited to a particular time or a particular place. When we begin to understand this, we begin to see God everywhere. And if we can see God everywhere, we stand a better chance of experiencing His love and comfort when and where we need it most.

28

"*Who loves a garden still his Eden keeps, / Perennial pleasures plants, and wholesome harvest reaps.*"
—Amos Bronson Alcott

I'm not good with gardening, but I recognize its merits. Brother Flavian toils in our rock garden and people come from all over to see it, even to have their picture taken in it. Brother James is refurbishing the garden in a courtyard where people often sit under the cloister walk when it rains, watching the water bead on the lush green life. And although I tend to have an ill-effect on plants of any kind, there is something to be said about a garden, and so I am grateful for the presence of the gardeners among us. Besides the beauty that exists in gardens, they are living proof of something we all need to remember from time to time: life can spring from even the most barren of patches, if we but care for it. What a merit there is in this indeed.

"One crowded hour of glorious life / Is worth an age without a name."
—Thomas Osbert Mordaunt

As I write this I have a terrible cold, and have to stop writing every three minutes or so to blow my nose. I am behind schedule on this book you are now reading, and have been working rather late hours for some time to try and get it finished. The skies are turning nearly black with clouds, and the wind is picking up, making me think that most certainly an ugly storm is on its way. It is not, in short, a good day.

At the same time, every fifteen minutes I hear the bells chime, and no matter how often I hear them, they're still lovely. There is a seminarian walking down the hall outside my office whistling what sounds to me like Beethoven's lovely Emperor Concerto. And all of it goes in to the mix to make me realize that—even in the darkest of days—goodness is all around.

"Moses, hearing the voice from the burning bush, said to God: 'Who am I that I should go to Pharaoh and lead the Israelites out of Egypt?'"

—Exodus 3:11

Who am I? he said, eyes and hands stretched to heaven in either gesture of praise or a shrug. I am one person. I have my own problems, my pastures to look over, my own sheep to tend to, my wounds to heal. I am not sure I can do what it is you want me to do. I'm not sure I can go on like you want me to. And to all of his concerns, God gave the answer: I will be with you. And He was.

Who am I, we may ask, our hands stretched to heaven in either a gesture of praise or one that just might resemble a shaking fist. I am one person. I have my own problems, I am trying to navigate through these dark pastures of grief where I find myself. I'm not sure I can go on like you want me to. And to all of our concerns, God gives his answer: I will be with you. And He is.

"No longer shall your name be Abram, but your name shall be Abraham."

—Genesis 17:5

"I will *never* call you Alaric," a friend told me, after I received my new name at the profession of monastic vows. And I understand that changing one's name is difficult for people to understand. The notion of beginning a new phase of a relationship with God (like Abram/Abraham) is not an easy one to grasp, and so many of us monks have to be content, I suppose, with wondering who in our life is going to call us what.

The fact remains, however, that growing closer to God *can* change us in a fundamental way. And, although we needn't necessarily desire to change our name, perhaps it would serve us well to change some of the adjectives we use to describe ourselves, as we change from "sinner" to "forgiven;" "grieving" to "understanding;" "lonely" to "lover."

NOVEMBER

"O Lord, I want to be in that number / When the saints go marching in."
—American Spiritual

We've had fat saints and skinny saints; we've had serious saints and saints with great senses of humor; we've had poor saints and rich saints; we've had saints with ordinary names like Mark, John, Elizabeth, and Mary, and saints with names that are a bit more out of the ordinary, like Fidelis of Sigmaringen, Fedlimid, Guthlake, Odo, and Odilo.

As different as the saints were, they all had one similarity: they all believed that Jesus was Lord and they tried their best to follow Him in all they did. They made mistakes, they might have faltered now and then, but they all tried to follow Him and constantly keep Him and the Faith in their hearts and minds. And those who do this, the Lord promises, will be blessed by him for all eternity.

2

"One day a farmer went out sowing. Part of what he sowed landed on a footpath ..."

—Matthew 13:3

You never know, Jesus seems to be telling us in this parable. You never know, given the right climate, the right soil, the right amount of rainfall, if something just might come of it.

And so, our smallest actions could bring about great results. Our little gestures at moving through grief to acceptance might not seem like a great deal at first, but if we have faith that the Lord can provide the correct climate, soil and rainfall, we can believe that our smallest efforts can yield more than we would have ever imagined.

"I look upon every day to be lost, in which I do not make a new acquaintance."

—Samuel Johnson

I met Ellen at—of all places—a monastery in France. I went there to study Gregorian chant, but much more seemed to happen than that. I walked away from the experience with a new friend, someone whose views on life I find interesting, and who doesn't mind listening to my own views.

I met Neal at my monastery. I was meeting him to give him an interview on Gregorian chant, but much more happened than that. I walked away from the experience with a new friend, someone whose take on life is just different enough from mine to make it interesting, and similar enough to make it compatible.

God continually sends people into our lives. If we do not see them as extensions of His care for us, we are missing a great deal of grace.

4

"What wisdom can you find that is better than kindness?"

—Jean Jacques Rousseau

Her name was Kristy, and I knew very little about her. I knew she was the only other second grader who seemed to have an appreciation of the Beatles akin to my own, since she brought Beatles albums for show and tell three times. I knew she was of a different religious background than most of the people at my school, since she couldn't say the Pledge of Allegiance and had to leave during Halloween parties. I knew she was what we called then one of the "slow" kids, since she went to reading with a different teacher.

And then one day, months after my mother had died, she asked me if I missed her, something no one else in my class had done. When I told her I did, she offered me a fun-size candy bar, and in this little act of kindness I saw that I knew a great deal more about her than I thought.

"God is love—I dare say. But what a mischievous devil Love is!"

—Samuel Butler

When I was a junior in high school I fell in love for the first time, with a girl named Nancy. There was something terribly urgent about the whole affair, and this mysterious love seemed to infect every aspect of my life. In English class it seemed to me that Macbeth was so tragic because he just hadn't really found the right woman. At the dinner table I would stare dreamily into my mashed potatoes, wondering what she was eating at her house, longing for the end of supper when I could call her and ask her myself. Every aspect of life seemed charged with an excess of energy.

When I read that God is love, I think sometimes it bears more resemblance to this urgent kind of love than the more civilized, polite love with which we often equate God.

6

"Love truth, but pardon error."

—Voltaire

One Thanksgiving when my niece Kristen was a little girl, she knocked a crystal goblet off the table, causing it to break against the leg of a chair. Her response to her mother's stern stare was, "I only wanted to help!" And of course, she meant no harm, and was quickly forgiven.

It may be that there are loved ones who have contributed to parts inside of us where we sense brokenness. These faults can seem multiplied and worsened after their death, because there seems to be no way of addressing the hurt that was caused. There is perhaps nothing that can put all the pieces back together, but praying for the grace to forgive can at least help us remember the beauty that was once part of the crystal.

"I bend but do not break."
—Jean de La Fontaine

"How much more can one man take?" the psalmist questions, and it is a question that has been on the lips of many ever since. There are those people to whom suffering and hardship seem to be attracted like metal to a magnet. For these people (and maybe we would at times count ourselves among their number) there seems to be no escaping the suffering that hovers over and around them. How much can people take?

Although the answer to this question perhaps cannot be stated in a demonstrable way, an answer can be stated nonetheless: God will not allow us to take on more than we can handle. This doesn't always seem like the best answer to us—indeed, it can seem far from it—but when we're bending, it's the only answer there is.

> *"If we had no winter, the spring would not be so pleasant: if we did not sometimes taste of adversity, prosperity would not be so welcome."*
>
> —Anne Bradstreet

It can be a little trite, this notion that we wouldn't be able to fully appreciate the goodness of life without experiencing its loss, and there are probably times—such as in the midst of dark moments—where not many of us would subscribe to it. But there is clearly something here. Those moments in our lives where we suffer—like it or not—do temper us, do change our outlook on life.

How this can be a comfort in the midst of our suffering, however, remains—at least to me, anyway—a mystery. But it's a mystery not unworthy of spending my life figuring out. Much like the mystery of the Cross, to which it is bound.

"A thousand ages in Thy sight / Are like an evening gone."

—Isaac Watts

Father Theodore is 99 years old, and one of the holiest people I know. He never misses prayer; he never seems to get too upset when things around him don't go perfectly; he always has a smile to offer in the corridor. I'm not sure if Father Theodore was this holy as a young man—indeed, no one is, as he has outlived anyone who could tell. But I would have to think that some of his holiness comes from being able to put things in a larger perspective. What seems so absolutely pressing to us right now, just may not with the passage of time, although we have a hard time believing that. But we must believe it, we who profess to honor One who is Lord of all the ages.

"Lord save us! We are lost!"

—Matthew 8:25

Once, as a freshman in college on a weekend trip to Chicago, my friends and I got so lost that we ended up miles and miles into Indiana and didn't even know it. Chicago is a wonderful yet aggravating city, and, even though we had a map, the streets there didn't at the time seem to go straight. And, if they did go straight, they seemed to change names in the middle of the street.

Life, especially a life marked by loss, can seem much the same way. We long for a road map to help us know how to get through and around obstacles, only to find that the ways are crooked and just may change on us in the middle of the road. Our only hope, our only map, is Jesus Christ, who travailed the ways of sorrow and suffering Himself, and so most certainly knows how to show us where we need to go.

*"Zaccheus he / Did climb the tree /
Our Lord to see."*

—The New England Primer

I frequently say that if a seven-foot-tall woman with a bee-hive hairdo wants to see a movie, not only will she choose the same movie that I am seeing, but will most likely sit in the seat in front of me. Life is filled with those obstacles that can get in the way of what our vision truly should be. But all too often, we get so caught up in the obstacle, that we can quit trying to see what we should.

Not so with Zaccheus. His solution to not being able to see the Lord (who should, of course, be the destination of all our hopeful glances) was to climb above anything that would obscure his vision. And he was rewarded for it. As shall we.

12

*"I cannot reach it, and my striving eye
/ Dazzles at it, as at eternity."*

—Henry Vaughan

"Your mother's in heaven now" I heard more times than I could possibly count in the weeks following her death. And I couldn't quite grasp what that meant, because I thought of my mother as I had always known her—a warm, living person of flesh and blood, and I was quite unsure what this spirit-world place was supposed to be about. And so all those proclamations of my mother's presence there really did little to comfort me.

But I did feel comfort on my Dad's lap, answering questions that I know had to be painful to hear. I felt comfort as my sister rubbed my feet. I felt comfort in my grandma's arms, calling me her "Baby." And I soon discovered that if I wanted to fully understand the dazzling love of heaven, I need only look around at the dazzling love I felt here, on earth. And it made heaven all that more accessible.

"A man who has nothing can whistle in a robber's face."

—Juvenal

There are those who talk about poverty in terms of people not being able to have their basic needs met, and—obviously—how we need to be about the business of making sure that more people get what they need and deserve. There are those relatively few in number who talk about poverty as a good thing, about the only way to true happiness coming by way of detachment. Many, perhaps, would say that this latter notion of poverty is best left to monks and nuns.

I would disagree. Whereas we all need to work to eradicate the first kind of poverty, I think, too we all need to embrace the second kind of poverty, however that may look in the individual circumstances of our lives. Because if we are truly poor, then we are in a better mindset to accept what we have been given and recognize it comes from God.

"The time to be happy is now, / The place to be happy is here, / The way to be happy is to make others so."

—Robert Green Ingersoll

When I was in college, sitting in a particularly boring lecture, I would look at the classroom door and imagine someone coming in and telling that he was sent here by the Pope, and needed me to come with him to Rome because John Paul had a delicate mission that he could entrust only to me. Or he would tell me that he was sent there by Paul McCartney, and the three surviving Beatles had decided that they wanted to get back together and replace John with me. Before long, the time would come for the class to be over and I would scurry out into the hall, clueless as to what we had just been discussing.

The Pope or the Beatles have never called me, and now I wonder how much more I could have learned, have grown, if I had paid attention to the moment, and not wished it away.

"Who has seen the wind? / Neither you nor I: / But when the trees bow down their heads, / The wind is passing by."

—Christina Georgina Rossetti

Once I was talking to a class of second graders. We were supposed to talk about religion, but as is the delightful way of second graders, topics tend to be a bit less constrictive, and the planned topic was broadened to include my dog, their dogs, hamsters, pizza, and Nintendo.

Eventually, however, I was able to steer things back to religion, and the question was asked of how we knew there was a God. I tried to talk about faith—just *knowing* somehow—but wasn't getting through to them. Just then, a kid shouted out that he knew there was a God because his dad took him to see the Cardinals play once and bought him a soda, even though his mother said before they left not to have any soda, it would keep him up all night. I didn't quite see the connection, but the lad seemed to get knowing nods from his classmates.

16

"I give you a heart so wise and understanding that there has never been anyone like you up to now, and after you there will come no one to equal you."

—I Kings 3:12

God approached Solomon with an amazing offer: Ask something of me and I will give it to you. Imagine how enormous that offer was. Like Aladdin's famous genie, God was granting absolutely anything. And for what did Solomon wish? Wisdom, an understanding heart.

How much easier life would be if, instead of trying to wish away sorrow, we would instead seek to understand it— and our God and each other—better.

"*Then he left them, got into the boat again, and went off to the other shore.*"

—Mark 8:13

We are taught: "If at first you don't succeed, try, try again." And this is sage advice for just about any area of life. We must face our struggles with fierce determination, with perseverance. There is grace in the struggle, we know, so we should stick with it.

There is also grace in knowing when we need to step away from the struggle, however. Losing ourselves in a beautiful piece of music, taking a walk, reading a book, seeing a movie can help us put things in perspective, and maybe the struggle won't look so monumental from the other shore.

18

"When a thought takes one's breath away, a lesson on grammar seems an impertinence."

—Thomas Wentworth Higginson

These words were written to introduce the poetry of Emily Dickinson. Dickinson's poetry is wondrous, mad, exhilarating, gut-wrenching, and oh-so-alive. People who took too great a pain talking about the oddities of her grammar, meter, and punctuation were completely missing the picture of the greatness of her work.

It is a tendency for all of us to concentrate so much on the punctuation and rules of grammar that we miss the breathtaking grandeur of the poem. If we think that we know God and what He wants from us only from concentrating on rigid rules and formulae, then we are not taking into account the life-changing beauty of His Word, which—contrary to all rules of grammar—is spoken without any punctuation at all, but goes on forever.

"Let each man think himself an act of God, / His mind a thought, his life a breath of God."

—Philip James Bailey

I was practicing the organ in the church one day, when a family came in—a mother, father, and a child that looked to be about three years of age. I ceased playing for a while, so that they could have a little silence to accompany their discovery of the church, and as I watched them, I encountered a marvelous sight: the three-year-old had discovered that if she made a noise in the church, the noise continued on seconds after she ceased making it. What sheer delight this discovery produced in her, and what embarrassment for her parents, as they tried to get her stop filling the silent church with noise.

What a lovely image, I reflected later, on the sheer continuity of the breath of God present in us all. Nothing can silence the Word that that breath produced, and it continues long after it is spoken.

"A kind mouth multiplies friends, and gracious lips prompt friendly greetings."

—Sirach 6:5

"I vant to be alone" Greta Garbo (or was it Talullah Bankhead?) purred and we all know, at times, what that desire is all about. There are times when the rigors of life have so accumulated that the presence of people in our lives— even family and friends—can make us feel crowded, irritable. And, often, before we can even think about it, we have said harsh or thoughtless words, perhaps desiring to make *someone* pay for the strife that is whirling inside of us. And harsh and thoughtless words can bring about hurt feelings.

It is no crime to want to be alone every now and then, and it is certainly no crime to purr that to our own loved ones. It's just better to purr than to roar.

"*When the water was thus divided, the Israelites marched into the midst of the sea on dry land, with the water like a wall to their right and to their left.*"

—Exodus 14:22

Not long after I began writing this book, I was in a bookstore and decided to look at what offerings were available on grief and loss. I picked up one book, written by a psychologist, and in it she spoke of grief using prepositions like "around" and "over." She's the expert, I understand, and there is something to be said about the psychological necessity of maneuvering around our grief, and getting over our grief, but I'm not sure in the end I agree with her model.

What model would I offer in its stead? The model of the people of Israel, who knew that the only sure way to freedom was to go *into the midst* of the dark waters, surrounded by all that could crush them. It's risky, of course, but the outcome is nothing short of the Promised Land.

22

"We don't see the end of the tunnel, but I must say I don't think it is darker than it was a year ago, and in some ways lighter."

—John Fitzgerald Kennedy

There are few people of a certain age who can't recall exactly where they where when they heard the news. The very world was rocked to its core: a nation had lost a leader; a family had lost a son; and the world itself seemed to lose some of its light. The unthinkable had happened; how could we move on? The question has been asked again and again when other families have lost their children, when the worlds of others have seen a diminishment in light: How can we move on?

His own words serve as the answer. We go forward, bit by bit, and realizing that the tunnel around us is dark, and, indeed, may be dark for some time to come. But perhaps we will slowly come to understand that the light at the end is getting bigger.

"*Then one of them, seeing that he was healed, turned back, praising God with a loud voice; and he fell on his face at Jesus' feet, giving him thanks.*"

—Luke 17:15-16

He had to give thanks. One encounter with the man Jesus Christ, and suddenly, he was whole, healed, and his life would never be the same. Before, if he were to reflect on his life, it would be nothing but a vision of cruel possibilities, each scenario played out in his mind like music out of tune—grating, cacophonous, disturbing. But that had changed. Life now played itself out with realities that had never been a part of his world before: hope, light, life, love. The others with him on his journey might not agree, but he had to give thanks. He knew, ultimately, that the thanksgiving was an integral part of the cure.

"*They partook of food with glad and generous hearts, praising God and having favor with all the people.*"

—Acts 2:46-47

They had to give thanks. Gathered in homes and cemeteries, our ancestors in the Christian faith recognized that an encounter with Jesus had so changed them that they would never be the same. And so they gathered to give thanks. In a world that was hostile to their message, that could strip them of their very life and dignity just for professing His name, they nevertheless gathered, and in rooms around their world gathered to sing songs, to praise the goodness of their Savior, and to break bread as He commanded them to do. They had to give thanks. They knew, ultimately, that thanksgiving was an integral part of being nourished.

"I thank you God, with all my heart."
—Psalm 137

Even in our darkest moments, I think we, too, need to know how important it is to give thanks. We are aware that our encounters with Jesus can so change us that we too, even in the midst of a world that can still be hostile to His message, know hope, light, life, love. The blessings of this world are mere reflections of those encounters, and we must always strive to mirror the praise of that leper, of those early Christians, of all who have been touched by His presence, by his love. And so, we too, must give thanks. We know, ultimately, that giving thanks is an integral part of living.

*"My marks and scars I carry with me,
to be a witness for me, that I have
fought His battles who now will be my
rewarder."*

—John Bunyan

My first trip to the beach—one of
my favorite places on earth—after
my last two major surgeries filled me
with great dread. In order to bask in the
warmth of the sun I would have to
expose my rather significant scars for all
the world to see. I saw them as ugly,
these scars, and wanted to hide them.
But the lure of the sun was too grand for
me to ignore, and so to the beach I went.

I was walking along, rather self-con-
sciously, when an older gentleman
approached me, pointed to my stomach
and exclaimed, "That's quite a scar you
have there, buddy!" He then unbuttoned
his own shirt, showed me a scar of his
own and said, "They're beautiful, aren't
they? It shows we've survived."

He was right, of course, about those
scars, and about the ones that aren't
readily visible to the eye.

> "*If one blind man leads another, both will end in a pit.*"
>
> —Matthew 15:14

There are as many ways to deal with grief and loss as there are perhaps people in the world. Books and pamphlets have been written, seminars given, sermons preached that help people who are awash in grief to somehow make sense of it all. And it is a good thing there are so many ways, because different people need different things.

Not all the ways are good ways. People who try to escape their grief through sedating it somehow are ultimately not helping themselves. Nor are people who ignore their grief, act like it doesn't exist. And so, whereas many who have gone this road before us can serve as our guides, many cannot, for nothing comes of the blind leading the blind, except for darkness.

"He endows man with a strength of his own, and with power over all things else on earth."

—Sirach 17:3

Bosnia. Croatia. Rwanda. Chechnya. The list goes on and on, of places where people have suffered debilitating tragedies, where famine and violence and death and suffering seem to go hand in hand with the very names of the places themselves, as if you can't really say any of the places without onerous adjectives hovering nearby to modify them.

But even if the names, now so familiar, are of pieces of land far away, the names are essentially of people—people exactly like you and me, who have the same vision and hope that we have. People who cry out to make sense of it all. People who—perhaps most amazingly—survive it all: the degradation, the strife, the utter desolation. And in the midst of it all, in the midst of the suffering, is a God who has given them strength. And that strength is ours as well.

"God's mill grinds slow, but sure."
—George Herbert

W e'll feel better some day, we're told, God will see to it. And then we look around the world and see all kinds of people starving whom God is supposed to be caring for; we see people shackled in darkness, longing for, but not receiving, the light of mercy. We see these things and we wonder: if God is tending to these people, why isn't more being done? It doesn't bode well for us, who are weighted down by our own sorrows.

It is faith, pure and simple, that allows us to see that God is tending to these people, He is there in the suffering, He is there among the poverty, He is there with the captives longing to be free, He is there in our sorrow. We may not approve of His timeline, but faith tells us that what He wills, and not our own will, is of the ultimate importance. And so we wait and hope, as God's mill grinds on.

N
O
V
E
M
B
E
R

"When the disciples approached Jesus, they asked him, 'Why do you speak to them in parables?'"

—Matthew 13:10

I'm not sure, as a young boy, if I would have understood what it really meant to be a part of a family that extended beyond my own, if it weren't for my Gramps, and the stories he told of his days growing up, of his parents and brothers and sisters who—I realized— were my great-grandparents and great aunts and uncles. I am not sure I would have felt a connection to my father's youth had he not told me stories of his days on the farm. Yes, as a boy, I figured out who I was and where I came from through listening to the stories of those around me.

If we are having difficulty understanding loss in our lives, perhaps we could turn to the story of the man Jesus, and find in Him not only insights into suffering and loss, but learn who we are and where we came from.

DECEMBER

"Every worthwhile gift, every genuine benefit comes from above, descending from the father of the heavenly luminaries, who cannot change and who is never shadowed over."

—James 1:17

Before my mother died, at Christmas time, we presented her with a mother's ring, with one stone each for her three children. As she opened the small box she was overcome with emotion, and began weeping intensely. I was just a small boy, and I didn't understand how getting a gift—one that she obviously liked—could bring about these tears that usually were reserved for bad things like pain and frustration. Maybe it wasn't such a good gift after all, I thought.

I know now, in a way I could have never known then, that gifts are about more than just feeling good. Gifts are about offering a part of who we are—complete with pain—to those whom we love. Viewed in this light, even her very tears ended up being a gift.

"There is cause for rejoicing here."

—1 Peter 1:6

What an amazing statement of faith this is. Peter is writing of trials and sufferings that his flock may have to endure, of death and fear and confusion. And, he is telling them, even in the midst of death and fear and confusion, they have cause for rejoicing. It seems a little optimistic at best, and downright crazy at worst. But Peter obviously believes it, and expects his flock to believe it as well, regardless of the cost.

And so this proclamation is given to us as well. And we are expected to believe it, regardless of the cost. Optimistic? Most definitely. Crazy? Perhaps. But we've most likely rejoiced over crazier things than this.

"We pardon to the extent that we love."

—François, Duc de Rochefoucauld

I had to face it, eventually, the anger I felt towards my mother. It would crop up on days like the Friday before Mother's Day, when my grade school classmates would be busy making something beautiful for their mothers, and I had to do something for my father or sister instead. It would crop up on those first few birthdays, when hers was not among the faces sitting around the table. And every time it would crop up, I would tell myself that it was wrong to be angry with her—it wasn't her fault that she died—but the anger was there nonetheless.

But deep within myself I have had to learn not to be angry with myself, and not to be angry with her: both of us have done what we could. And this release, this pardon, comes from nothing less than the love we shared, and continue to share in some way.

3

D
E
C
E
M
B
E
R

4

"Moses said to the people: 'Did anything so great ever happen before?'"
—Deuteronomy 4:32

Every now and then we need to hear it, whether we want to or not. Every now and then, we need to sit down and make ourselves realize just what amazing things God has done in this world, even if we are having a hard time seeing it right now. Because the fact remains that indeed nothing so great ever *did* happen before. God sent His Son into the world to lead captive souls into freedom, and because of His death and resurrection, we know that those whom we love who have gone before us have union with Him as a reality in a way that the people of Moses' day just did not. We need to hear it.

*"Jesus spoke thus: 'Come to me, all you
who are weary and find life burden-
some, and I will refresh you.'"*

—Matthew 11:28

I was never supposed to drink straight
out of the bottle, but I always did. In
the refrigerator, as soon as you opened
the door, was an old orange juice bottle
that we kept filled with water. On summer days, after having been hard at the
work of play, I could hardly wait to rush
into the coolness of the kitchen, feel the
icy blast of air as I opened the refrigerator door, and reached for the bottle.
Who had time to go to the cabinet, get
a glass, pour it in the glass, and politely
return the bottle to the refrigerator?
Certainly not I, who relished the cool
refreshment even as it spilled over my
quaking chin and collected in a puddle
on the floor.

Jesus desires to refresh us so. Let us
never forget this, even in the midst of
the heat.

"With God all things are possible."
—Mark 10:27

We don't always believe it, this business of all things being possible with God. We can recount all the wonders God has done in the past; we can get all misty-eyed as lisping third-grade angels announce the birth of the Messiah, while antsy shepherds with towels on their heads shift nervously nearby; we can wax eloquently about that empty tomb, with the sun rising behind it and the Hallelujah Chorus ringing out its glorious polyphony.

But all that is in the past. What about now? What about the possibility of God taking that within us that hurts and making it whole, healed? What about the possibility that, not only can God heal us, He can take that which has made us hurt in the first place and make it an instrument of our healing. How bizarre. But how entirely possible, with this great God of the impossible.

"Because God's gifts put man's best dreams to shame."

—Elizabeth Barrett Browning

Who would have dreamed of it, a world filled with light and darkness, land and water, fish and fowl, men and women? God would have, that's who, He who said: Let there be light. Who would have dreamed of it, a virgin giving birth to a child? God would, that's who, He who received Mary's word: Let it be done unto me according to your word. Who would have dreamed of it, a man broken, beaten, and killed, rising from the dead? God would, that's who, He who inspired the words: He has risen, as He said He would.

And the list is nearly endless of the amazing gifts that God has bestowed and continues to bestow upon us, His awe-filled people. And the point needs to be acknowledged over and over again: let us never assume that just because we can't imagine something, God can not; for His dreams continue to make life happen.

8

"*The reign of God is like a buried treasure which a man found in a field.*"
—Matthew 13:44

I recently received an e-mail from a friend I hadn't spoken to in years. We hadn't had any kind of a falling out, it's just that time and distance took its toll and we lost touch. Then, quite unexpectedly, I heard from him, and it was a wonderful surprise, a treasured discovery.

Life can be filled with such surprises, if we keep our eyes open for them. And finding these treasures can help make sure that moments of sorrow never completely bury moments of joy.

"Return, rebellious children, says the Lord."

—Jeremiah 3:14

Once, when my brother and I were roughhousing, he accidentally put his foot through an aquarium, causing slimy water and fish cascading out all over the floor. Aware that our father was going to hit the roof, and having seen too many Saturday matinees on Channel 11 where the falsely accused man is given shelter by an understanding friar, we hopped on our bikes and rode to the church, allowing the quiet of its space to quiet our own fractured breathing. Eventually, however, we knew we would have to return home to face the music.

It can be our first response to escape those things in our lives that cause us discomfort, pain, or fear and escape for a while can provide a necessary respite, a quiet place to think. But escape is not a solution. Reluctantly, we need to face the music, even if it sounds like a dirge.

10

"Long is the way / And hard, that out of hell leads up to light."

—John Milton

I live on a hill, a fact which is quite enjoyable when I am going out for a bicycle ride, but lamentable upon my return. Legs burning, breath heaving, I make my ascent, willing myself not to get off my bike and take the easier mode of walking. I can do this, I tell myself, regardless of the fact that I am out of shape, that my legs burn and it feels as if my chest is about to explode. And when I arrive at the top, I don't have any enormous feeling of accomplishment; I don't prance around Rocky-like while stirring music swirls around me. No, when you live on a hill, you have to expect that there are going to be all kinds of uphill climbs, and just be about the business of getting up there.

Life, it seems, is no different.

*"Are you not from eternity, O Lord,
my holy God, immortal?"*

—Habakkuk 1:12

11

D
E
C
E
M
B
E
R

Time can be as varied as the circumstances in which it presents itself. Sitting in a dentist's chair, mouth agape and filled with tools, a few minutes can seem to last much longer. The same time can seem to rush by if we are spending it eating our favorite desert, feeling the taste of the last bite slowly dissipate from our mouths. Time, it seems, is relative.

Which is a good insight when pondering of the nature of sorrow and suffering in our lives. God is eternal, and though it seems like we can at times suffer for an eternity, we know that it is but an instant in God's eyes. And the only way to make that instant more bearable for us, whose perception of time can be sometimes languorous, sometimes swift, is to make it our constant prayer that we may see more and more as God sees.

12

*"The soul's dark cottage, batter'd and
decay'd, / Lets in new light through
chinks that Time has made."*

—Edmund Waller

Recently, while preaching a parish
mission, a woman came up to me
and said that, young as I was, it was
obvious I possessed an old soul. At the
time, I wasn't sure if the appropriate
response was "Thank you," or "I do not!"
The more I thought about it, however,
the more I decided it was a compliment.
I would like to think that the things that
have happened in my life—good and
bad—have perhaps wizened my soul
beyond my years. I am comforted by the
thought that, though I may be young or
immature or downright goofy, there is a
part of me that is beyond all that.

The same can probably be said of all
of us. The experiences of our lives have
affected us in the depths of our souls in
ways that we may not realize. The only
way to make sense of it all, is to be open
to that Light which comes from above to
illumine us with insight, with openness.

"This is the salvation which the prophets carefully searched out and examined."

—1 Peter 1:10

They left no stone unturned, those prophets of old. God told them to speak, and as their mouths opened to utter His marvelous poetry, they themselves looked for clues to the nature of life and love in the very words that came out. They wondered what God had in store for them, what amazing and terrible things would come to pass for those whom He had chosen. And the clues to it all were on their own lips, as they spoke of wonders that they themselves could only begin to imagine.

What they could only imagine, we can know. Because what was promised by the prophets so long ago has been fulfilled. And if we want to know what God has in store for us, what amazing and terrible things will come to pass for us, we must listen to their words and listen to the ultimate Word, Jesus Christ. We need search and examine no further.

"Appear not before the Lord empty-handed, for all that you offer is in fulfillment of the precepts."

—Sirach 35:4

"Offer it up" used to be a phrase that sprung often from the lips of Catholics whenever they had to endure something unattractive, ranging from something as enormous as one of life's major tragedies to something as ordinary as a trip to the dentist. The notion is that when we must endure something that we would rather not, we can link our pain to the pain of the Cross, and so make it a prayer to God.

Some would say this is old-fashioned, but I would disagree. If we believe that everything that happens to us in life can, in the end, be some mysterious gift from God, then it goes to follow that when we receive one of these gifts—*especially* when we can't quite see the gift nature of it—we need to offer it back to God. It is only through this offering that we can begin to see how varied God's gifts are.

"*There was a man named John sent by God to testify to the light, so that through him all might believe—but only to testify to the light, for he himself was not the light.*"

—John 1:6-8

How exciting he must have been, John the Baptist. Clad in camel's hair and leather, munching away on grasshoppers, he must have made quite a sight—a figure that, like Errol Flynn, might make women swoon and men want to be like him. I imagine his voice had to be thunderous and deep, and perhaps set him apart more than anything else. It was that voice that the prophet Isaiah had foretold thousands of years before, that made people look at their world and its possibilities a bit differently—to imagine a world where the lowly receive glad tidings, the brokenhearted are healed, and captives receive liberty. It was that voice that made people sit up and take note that their world was about to change forever. It was that voice that, if we listen to it, can still call us to imagine our world differently, and even heal our broken hearts.

"*The voice of one crying in the wilderness: Prepare the way of the Lord, make his paths straight.*"

—Matthew 3:3

There are those who would say that it is unfortunate that we don't have in our world today a figure like John the Baptist. There are those who would say that above the clamor and din of this world, no voice rises to show us the way as he did so many years ago. I don't believe that. Because, you see, the same Lord whom John foretold will come again. This has been promised to us, this we believe. And just as John's voice rang out with the possibilities of accepting an encounter with the one who is to save us, just as John's voice rang out with notions of what we can do to prepare for that coming, so too, I believe, there are voices in our world today calling out the same ideas. We need only listen to these voices, wherever we may encounter them.

"I will place my law within them, and write it upon their hearts."

—Jeremiah 31:33

For months after the death of my mother I would cry myself to sleep and wonder when I would feel better. I overheard someone say in reference to me, "His poor little heart is broken," and I figured that's what was wrong. How then, could I fix it? What could mend my heart? The answers didn't seem to be coming.

In retrospect, however, I realize that every time someone around me reached out to me, every time someone voiced their love, every time I was allowed to feel—if only for a moment—that things were good in the world, my heart was healing, gently caressed by a God for whom all those people were instruments. I know now what a solace it can be to recognize that caring touch when it's happening.

"That many people read a song / Who will not read a sermon."

—Winthrop Mackworth Praed

My friend David teases me about finding some of the answers to life's basic questions in the lines of pop songs, and I have to admit that it is something I tend to do—shallow as that may seem. I'm convinced that people who are inspired to write truly good music and lyrics are inspired by the same Spirit who hopefully helps me on my sermons. Whereas I may find Biblical allusions to help get across the notion of the beauty of love, does it not get across the same point when Peter Gabriel says that in someone's eyes he sees "the doorway to a thousand churches?"

And so if there is a song that seems to give voice to our grief, seems to speak to where we truly are, it's not necessarily shallow. It just could be the Spirit.

*"Now will I recall God's works; what
I have seen, I will describe."*

—Sirach 42:15

People who don't live in Chicago always seem to want to go to Rush Street when they are visiting. The area is filled with people, and—as is often the case with areas filled with people—activity that could best be described as perhaps not the moral ideal. And because of this, there are frequently street preachers perched on corners, yelling at people to reform their lives or else. Say what you will about their message, one has to respect their desire to yell the gospel message (or at least their take on it) to anyone who will listen.

There is something to be said about sharing our faith with others. Even if the faith we share is one filled with confusion, the proclaiming of it helps us understand it better, and can certainly help others.

20

"Many people were scolding him to make him keep quiet, but he shouted all the louder ..."

—Mark 10:48

There are times when our souls are filled with joy, and we wish to shout to the world of the wonders of creation. There are times when we are hurt, and we wish to shout to the world of our pain. There are times when we are perplexed, and we want to shout to the world of our search for the answers. There are times when we feel alone, and we want to shout to the world of our need for others.

And there are times when the world doesn't want to hear what we have to shout at it. It is at these times that we need to shout all the louder.

"O brave new world, / That has such people in't!"

—William Shakespeare

Father Godfrey, one of my oldest, dearest friends, is quite a piece of work. Hilarious and serious, pious and irreverent, aggravating and soothing, loquacious and listening, he has the ability to allow me to weep at my sorrows without ever letting the weeping have the final word, silencing it with the louder boisterousness of laughter.

People in our lives like Godfrey can't take sorrow away, but they can take a world clouded in mist and make it seem less dark somehow. They can serve as models to us that although we may weep, joy is all around us, ready to burst through into our lives, into our world at any moment. And what a great world it can be indeed, when we allow those who love us to help shape it.

"Abraham was the father of Jacob, and Jacob the father of Judah and his brothers ..."

—Matthew 1:2

A braham knew it, an emptiness. Called by God to be the father of a people, there was still something missing, still some distance between him and this mysterious God. And so when God told him to sacrifice his own son, he agreed to do so; maybe in hopes that this horrible ultimate act of love would fill the emptiness that must have been a part of him. God, we know, didn't allow him to carry through with it, but Abraham was willing, so strong was this emptiness. In the midst of it all, however—the searching, the longing, the confusion, the doubt—in the midst of it all, Abraham knew that only God could fill the emptiness. He need only wait for it to happen.

" ...And Salmon the father of Boaz by Rahab, and Boaz the father of Obed by Ruth ..."

—Matthew 1:5

Ruth knew it, this emptiness. Widowed and among a foreign people, she could have gone back to her own land, her own people. But she stayed with her mother-in-law, singing sweetly, "Wherever you go I will go, wherever you live I will live," these words of love trying to fill the emptiness that had to have been there. In the midst of it all, however—the searching, the longing, the confusion, the doubt—in the midst of it all, Ruth knew that only God could fill the emptiness. She need only wait for it to happen.

*" … And Obed the father of Jesse,
and Jesse the father of David the king."*
—Matthew 1:6

David the King knew it, this emptiness. Chosen as a youth to be Israel's king, bonded in a special covenant with God, he still longed to know him better, to be closer to him, singing, "To you, O Lord, I call; my rock, do not refuse to hear me, for if you are silent to me, I shall be like those who go down to the grave." David wrote many such psalms, but the emptiness remained. In the midst of it all, however—the searching, the longing, the confusion, the doubt—in the midst of it all, David knew that only God could fill the emptiness. He need only wait for it to happen.

" ... And Jacob the father of Joseph the husband of Mary, of whom Jesus was born, who is called Christ."

—Matthew 1:16

We have a lot in common with people like Abraham, Ruth, David, our ancestors. We, too, glimpse emptiness in our lives from time to time. But it is only a glimpse. If our ancestors knew the emptiness of questioning whether God was always present for them, we know the reality of One who was born into our very midst. If our ancestors knew the emptiness of questioning whether God really knew their pain, we know the reality of One like us, subject to suffering and pain, not immune to our struggles. And if our ancestors knew the emptiness of questioning whether God loved them, we know the reality of One who loved us so much that He willingly died for our sake, and left in His wake an empty tomb, to mock the emptiness that had once been present. Our emptiness can be filled. We need wait no longer.

"There is One who can protect you from a fall and make you stand unblemished and exultant in the presence of his glory."

—Jude 1:24

Some people turn to material objects, thinking that possessions alone can make life easier, more worthwhile. Some turn to events, as if merely keeping busy will quell any hungers that may be within them. Some turn to wrongdoing, as if doing something we know is wrong will help us feel right, if only for a moment. Whatever the case, the fact remains that all of us turn to all kinds of things to fill that which is empty inside of us, to make us forget loneliness, grief, sorrow.

The author of the letter of Jude perhaps understood the human nature that makes us chase after so much to try and make ourselves feel better. But he also knew the truth: all of it is in vain, for there is only One who can be all things for all people, quelling hungers, easing sorrow, inspiring exultation and glory.

"The attempt and not the deed con-founds us."

—William Shakespeare

Many have said that the hardest part of the particular style of praying with the Scriptures known as lectio divina (holy reading) is not the contemplation on the text, or the meditation, or even putting to words what we have gained from the experience, but just opening the Bible. Once the beginning is attempted, the rest usually flows a little easier.

So it is with the work of grief. There may be all kinds of things that we tell ourselves we need to do, all kinds of hurdles that we know await us that need to be jumped, but just setting our minds to the task and doing *something* is usually the hardest part. We need to be confident that, just as when we open the Bible we know that God can speak to us, so too He gently encourages us on to do what we must do, if we only open our minds to the beginning of the task.

"I rejoice heartily in the Lord, in my God is the joy of my soul; For he has clothed me with a robe of salvation and wrapped me in a mantle of justice."

—Isaiah 61:10

My mother had a blue velveteen robe with some sort of gold orphery on it that she frequently wore. I remember thinking as a child that it was a magnificent piece of clothing, and that she was like a beautiful queen when she wore it, regal and filled with strength. As I grew to adulthood, it was disappointing to look at photo albums where my mother is in the robe, because I could see that it was an ordinary robe, and that she was often frail and sickly in it.

Our memories of our loved ones can be clothed in all kinds of idealistic accoutrements, and it can be sad for us to acknowledge that things were not always necessarily as we perceived them. But the love that covers our memories, and the love with which God can clothe them now can indeed bring about rejoicing.

"You explain nothing, O poet, but thanks to you all things become explicable."

—Paul Claudel

I gave the address at a cancer survivor's day, and afterwards had the opportunity to discuss the disease with my fellow survivors. I was amazed at the amount of metaphor that was flying around the room like an excited bird: "I felt like a piece of luggage left at the airport that everyone kept looking into and putting back on the conveyor." "I felt like I had been invaded by an army with nothing to defend me." "I feel like I am constantly being followed by a thief, never knowing when he's going to mug me."

We may think that there is no one who feels the way we do, and to an extent we're right. But writers, poets, musicians, and painters have tried to express at least some of the human condition, and they just might have an idea of what we're experiencing if we listen to them.

30

"'Pass in, pass in,' the angels say, / 'In to the upper doors, / Nor count compartments of the floors, / But mount to paradise / By the stairway of surprise.'"
—Ralph Waldo Emerson

There are people who read the last page of the book first, and I have to be honest that these people clearly annoy me. It seems to me that part of the wonder of life is the finding out of things, and if we know the answer before the question gets really good and asked, then we're missing out on a great deal of where that question may take us. I understand that the unknown element of a surprise can be a risky venture, but there is clearly a pay-off in risking a surprise.

Definitely something to be remembered when we think we know all the answers, or can find them out. Our only real avenue of discovery lies in the surprise of God's love for us, and just where that may lead us is a mystery indeed.

"I am the Alpha and the Omega, the First and the Last, the Beginning and the End!"

—Revelation 22:13

For each ending, there is a beginning—such is the inescapable consequence of time. But to say this so facilely is not to give proper emphasis to the toll it takes on us, we who have to endure relinquishing the comfort of endings and step forth into the unfamiliarity of new beginnings. It is far from easy, this business of ending and beginning.

And the only way to endure it is to never lose sight of the One who is the beginning and end of all there is.

Let us renew ourselves to begin again in Him.